Ethics, Efficiency, and the Market

Ethics, Efficiency, and the Market

Allen Buchanan

University of Arizona

ROWMAN & ALLANHELD
PUBLISHERS

A portion of the essay "The Right to a Decent Minimum of Health Care," which appears in Chapter 3, pages 72–74, originally appeared in *Philosophy and Public Affairs*, volume 13, no. 1 (Winter 1984), and is reprinted here by permission of the Princeton University Press.

ROWMAN & ALLANHELD

Published in the United States of America in 1985
by Rowman & Allanheld, Publishers
(a division of Littlefield, Adams & Company)
81 Adams Drive, Totowa, New Jersey 07512

Library of Congress Cataloging in Publication Data
Buchanan, Allen E., 1948–
  Ethics, efficiency, and the market.
  (Rowman & Allanheld texts in philosophy)
  Bibliography: p.
  Includes index.
  1. Economics—Moral and ethical aspects. 2. Efficiency,
Industrial—Moral and ethical aspects. 3. Capitalism—
Moral and ethical aspects. I. Title. II. Series.
HB72.B83 1985   174'.4   84-27525
ISBN 0-8476-7395-2
ISBN 0-8476-7396-0 (pbk.)

85 86 87 / 10 9 8 7 6 5 4 3 2 1

Printed in the United States of America

For Deborah,
with love and thanks

Contents

Preface

I believe that this book will prove useful both to philosophers and economists, linking their distinctive approaches to the evaluation of the market. It is remarkable that political philosophers, past and present, devote so little thought to the problem of efficiency. In part this is only one instance of political philosophy's characteristic failure to take seriously the question of whether the ideals and principles it examines are practically attainable. The economists' failure to grapple with the problem of the ethical evaluation of social systems is equally remarkable, once the severe limitations of the standard of efficiency are fully appreciated.

I aim, however, at an even broader readership. It is my hope that this book will serve as an informative and provocative supplementary text for undergraduate and graduate students in courses on social and political philosophy, political theory, and economics. In particular, this book should be useful in political philosophy and political science courses that deal with theories of justice and with the debate between socialism and capitalism and in courses on the history of economics, comparative economic systems, ideology, philosophy of economics, and political sociology.

Every effort has been made to render technical issues, whether in ethics or in economics, as simply and clearly as accuracy permits. To further this pedagogical goal I have included a glossary of economic and philosophical terms.

Acknowledgments

I am indebted to a number of people who helped me in a variety of ways in writing this book. It was Baruch Brody who first encouraged me to write a long paper on the topic and then suggested that the paper might serve as the basis for a valuable short book. The Liberty Fund, Incorporated provided generous support for the paper.

All these people offered valuable comments on earlier drafts: Mary Anne Baily, James M. Buchanan, Dan W. Brock, David Friedman, Jules L. Coleman, Sam Gorovitz, Russell Hardin, Mark Isaac, Mark Kuperberg, Rolf Sartorius, and Edward Zajac. I am especially grateful to David Conn, Jody Kraus, and Julius Sensat, all of whom provided very important criticisms of early drafts. Deborah Mathieu contributed valuable comments throughout, suggesting many positive improvements. I also wish to express my appreciation to Marshall Cohen and Spencer Carr of Rowman & Allanheld Publishers for their cheerful encouragement and excellent editorial advice. Finally, I am grateful to Lois Day and Ann Hickman for their accurate and amiable work in preparing the manuscript for publication.

1

Introduction

The Aims of This Book

The subject indicated by the title of this book will seem to many to be overwhelmingly larger than the book itself. My aim, however, is not to execute an exhaustive study of all of the arguments that have been or could be presented for and against the market as a form of social organization. Such a task could not be completed in one volume, nor by one author. Nevertheless, it seems to me that there is a need for a short, clear, critical synthesis of the best thinking on what is undoubtedly one of the most important moral, social, and political issues of our time and of the foreseeable future: the controversy between those who defend the market and those who condemn it.

When described in very general terms, many of the arguments considered here will seem familiar. In each case, however, I have tried to present the most plausible version of the argument, as clearly and fairly as possible, and to articulate and examine its conceptual, normative, and empirical presuppositions. Instead of saying that I have attempted to present and criticize what is best in *the* literature that purports to evaluate the market, it would be more accurate to say that I have tried to bridge the gap between two distinct literatures, that of economics and that of normative ethics. The former has been dominated by attempts to assess the market solely on grounds of efficiency, to the neglect of ethical issues. Ethicists (and normative political theorists), on the other hand, have characteristically disdained considerations of efficiency (when they have thought about them at all), while concentrating on the moral assessment of the market, most recently in terms of its failure or success in satisfying the requirements of justice.

One of the most important conclusions of this book is that this sharp division of labor between ethicists and economists is untenable and rests upon the failure of both groups to reflect critically upon the presuppositions which underlie their respective approaches to the market. The adoption of the allegedly purely technical notion of efficiency that prevails in the economics literature itself rests upon controversial moral assumptions which I endeavor to make explicit and to criticize. Conversely, some of the most influential ethical arguments for and against the market rest on unarticulated assumptions about the efficiency or inefficiency of the market or rival systems. A major theme of this book is the complex and often inexplicit interplay between efficiency assessments and moral judgments. Another major theme is the precariousness of attempts to compare whole systems on grounds of efficiency. The charge of relativism has long been leveled at attempts to make comparative ethical judgments about different social systems; I shall argue that the problem of relativism for judgments of comparative efficiency is no less daunting.

In the literature of economics, political science, and philosophy, the phrase "the market" or "the market system" usually refers to *the market with private property in the means of production*. Even though there are systems of social organization within which the market plays a role in the absence of significant amounts of private property in the means of production, there are excellent reasons for focusing primarily upon the strengths and weakness of the private property market system. Historically, the overwhelming majority of those who have defended or attacked the market have either explicitly or implicitly assumed a significant if not a dominant role for private property in the means of production. But perhaps even more importantly, the private property market system at least in principle most closely approximates the theoretical ideal of the perfectly competitive market. It is true that the conditions for a perfectly competitive (and necessarily efficient) market are often stated without the assumption that property rights are rights of private, that is, individual ownership of the means of production (see chapter 1). What is important is the requirement that property rights (whether held by individuals or groups) are known and stable. Nonetheless, the more plausible systems which assign a significant role to markets in social organization but which exclude private property in the means of production, that is, the various types of market socialism, all include *in principle*, as well as in practice, certain conditions which explicitly violate one or more of the necessary conditions for a perfectly competitive market. For example, the more attractive and widely discussed versions of market socialism which feature worker control of competing firms also include roles for the central government in (a) determining patterns and rates of investment, and in (b) placing restrictions on how individual firms may use their capital resources. Both of these functions violate at least one necessary condition of the perfectly competitive market: that there is free entry into and exit from the market.

Since the market with private property in the means of production is historically and theoretically the dominant form of market system, it will be this kind of social organization that is referred to in what follows when the phrase "the market" or "the market system" is used, except where a distinction is explicitly drawn between the private property market system and some version of market socialism. The final chapter, however, examines market socialism and explores the question of how the attempt to sever the market from private property in the means of production affects moral and efficiency arguments for the market.

This book has two aims: first, to formulate clearly the most important arguments for and against the market as a mechanism for allocating resources and for producing and distributing goods and services; second, to assess these arguments, especially by critically examining their often unarticulated presuppositions. In many cases it will not be possible to adjudicate decisively between the conflicting arguments, in part because the outcome depends upon empirical data which are either unavailable or disputed. Indeed one of the more important contributions of such an investigation as this is to distinguish more clearly between those issues that in principle can be resolved by empirical research and those that cannot.

The Distinction Between Efficiency Arguments and Ethical Arguments

Arguments can be grouped under two headings: arguments for or against the market *on grounds of efficiency*, and arguments *on moral grounds*. In many cases this rough distinction is unproblematic. Some advocates of the market contend, for example, that only this form of social organization is compatible with respect for certain alleged natural rights, such as a right to private property or a right against coercion. Others make the case for the market solely on the grounds that it allocates resources and distributes products most efficiently, eschewing any attempt to establish its moral superiority. Evidently the two types of arguments can point in opposite directions. It is quite consistent to argue that the market is so morally defective that it ought to be reformed or even abandoned, even if doing so would result in a loss of efficiency. Similarly, one may acknowledge moral deficiencies of the market, and nonetheless consistently conclude that they are not so grave as to require us to forgo its efficiency in favor of a less efficient, but morally preferable system. We shall see, however, that many parties to the debate assert or assume a happy congruence between efficiency and moral values.

The Paretian Concept of Efficiency

The most widely accepted concept of efficiency is that developed by Vilfredo Pareto. A state of a given system is Pareto Optimal if and only if there is no feasible alternative state of that system in which at least one person is better off and no one is worse off. A state, S^1, is Pareto Superior to another state, S^2, if and only if there is at least one person who is better off in S^1 than in S^2 and no one is worse off in S^1 than in S^2. These are the most inclusive formulations of the Paretian principles.[1]

The Pareto Optimality and Pareto Superiority principles may be formulated more narrowly to refer exclusively to distributional states. In other words, taking a certain stock of consumer goods (including services) as given, we can ask whether a particular distribution of them, D, among the persons in the system is such that there is no alternative way of distributing those goods, D^1, among those individuals, that would make at least one individual better off without making anyone worse off (Distributive Pareto Optimality). And we can ask whether a change from one distribution (D^1) of a given stock of consumer goods among a set of persons to another distribution (D^2) would improve the condition of someone without worsening the condition of anyone else (Distributive Pareto Superiority).

On the other hand, the Principles of Pareto Optimality and Pareto Superiority can be applied not to distributions of consumer goods but instead exclusively to *allocations of resources for producing goods*. An allocation of productive resources is Pareto Optimal if and only if there is no (technically possible) alternative allocation which would produce more of at least one good without producing less of some other good (Productive Pareto Optimality). Similarly, if an allocational state, A, would produce more of at least one good than an allocational state, A^1, but without producing less of any other good than A^1, then allocational state A is Productively Pareto Superior to allocational state A^1. The more inclusive formulation of the Pareto Optimality and Pareto Superiority principles stated at the beginning of this section is broad enough to combine distributional allocational assessments if 'S^2' and 'S^1' are understood as referring to allocational-distributional states. An allocational-distributional state consists of both a given allocation of productive resources and a coexisting distribution of consumer goods (and services).

Economists sometimes distinguish yet another type of efficiency. A system is said to be Aggregatively Efficient if it employs all available productive resources; Aggregatively Inefficient if it does not. Critics of the market often argue that that system is Aggregatively Inefficient because it regularly suffers from unemployment—failure to utilize available labor. However, Aggregative Efficiency as it stands is an incomplete evaluative criterion for two reasons. First, what is important for the evaluation of a system is not whether a productive resource is being used but whether it is being used in an efficient way. The fact that certain resources are not being used need not constitute a significant defect of a system if they are not needed or if their use would be unproductive or inefficient. For these reasons it seems best to subsume Aggregative Efficiency under Productive Pareto Optimality. Thus unemployment (of potentially productive workers) would result in Productive Pareto Suboptimality only if putting the unemployed to work would result in the production of greater quantities of some goods without reducing the quantities produced of other goods. Further, even if certain idle resources could be used to produce a particular item, this will be of little consequence if the item that would be produced would not in fact increase anyone's well-being, either because the thing is not desired by anyone to whom it is distributed, or because it is not distributed to anyone who desires it, or because the resource is worth more than the product it would yield.

It is important to emphasize, of course, that inefficiency may not be the only complaint about unemployment—unemployment may be condemned on moral grounds; for example, because of its deleterious effects upon the self-esteem or self-respect of the unemployed. The main limitation on the usefulness of Aggregative Efficiency as a criterion for assessing social systems is that it does not include the appropriate connections between resources, productivity, and *benefits* from what is produced.

Notice that the notion of Productive Pareto Optimality suffers from a similar, though more limited shortcoming. By focusing only on the quantity of outputs attainable from a given set of inputs, Productive Pareto Optimality fails to engage the root idea behind the Pareto Optimality and Pareto Superiority principles: the effect of the particular form of social organization in question on the well-being of the individuals involved. For clearly a system would be Productively Pareto Superior to another without making anyone better off if the additional goods it produced made no contribution to anyone's well-being. For instance, the fact that system S can produce more nuclear weapons than system S^1 without reducing its production of other goods does little to establish the superior efficiency of system S if more nuclear weapons are of no benefit—unless we are willing to divorce the notion of efficiency from that of well-being entirely. This point will become important later when we examine attempts to compare the efficiency of rival systems by comparing their productivity.

A related but distinct conception of productive efficiency is what is commonly called productivity; that is, the ratio of outputs to inputs. One system is more productive than another in this sense if it produces a greater output than another, granted the same input. This second conception of productive efficiency differs from Productive Pareto Optimality insofar as it measures productivity relative to a constant resource base. The Productive Pareto Optimality Principle in contrast does not assume equal inputs.

Productivity, that is, productive efficiency as maximization of outputs relative to inputs, like Productive Pareto Optimality, has no necessary connection with well-being. A system S may produce more of a good G than a system S^1, using the same quantity of inputs I, yet no one will be better off in S than in S^1 unless the extra quantity of G brings an additional benefit to someone.

To compare two systems on grounds of productivity it is necessary to select some particular type of output or set of types of outputs (for example, steel and bread) that are common to both systems and compare the amounts of these produced in the two systems to some constant quantity of a type of input (or set of types of inputs) which is also common to the two systems. More importantly, it is also necessary to assume that the particular products (outputs) and resources (inputs) that provide the basis for the comparison are *equally valuable* to individuals in the two systems, if productivity comparisons are to be reliable indicators of comparative efficiency, and if we are to assume that efficiency has some relationship to how well off people are. For example, the fact that one system produces more guns per unit of iron than another is of limited interest if individuals in the two systems place sharply different values on guns. To assume that the products or resources identified in productivity comparisons have the same or roughly the same values for individuals in two different systems is to assume interpersonal utility comparisons, that is, comparisons of how well off one individual is relative to how well off another is.

For the same reason that productivity is inadequate for overall efficiency assessments, neither the growth rate, nor the rate of capital accumulation is by itself a satisfactory measure of a system's efficiency, unless we divorce the concept of efficiency from that of well-being. A system with a higher rate of accumulation or a higher growth rate might not make people better off, if it suffered from an inefficient distribution system, for example.

Among the efficiency principles discussed, the Pareto Optimality and Pareto Superiority principles appear to provide the most comprehensive tools for assessing a system's efficiency, since the notion of a social state they employ is inclusive enough to take into account the way productive resources are allocated, the way production is organized, and the distribution of consumer goods so far as all of these affect how well off individuals are. However, since the Pareto Optimality and Pareto Superiority principles focus only on the impact of these factors upon individual well-being, not upon the relative contributions which each factor makes to individual well-being, a judgment that a particular system is in a Pareto Suboptimal state or that one social state is Pareto Inferior to another by itself tells us nothing about whether the source of inefficiency lies in the allocation of productive resources among producers, in the ways in which production is actually organized, or in the mechanism for distributing what is produced. In what follows, the relevant notions of efficiency will most often be that of Pareto Optimality and Pareto Superiority, though in some instances the more specific Distributional or Productive Pareto Optimality and Superiority principles may be invoked.

The wide acceptance of the Pareto Optimality and Pareto Superiority principles is usually attributed at least in part to the fact that they provide a way of assessing social states that does not require *interpersonal utility* comparisons. While there is considerable, though not unanimous, agreement that interpersonal utility comparisons cannot be made, there has been sharp difference of opinion as to why they cannot be made. Some have contended that such comparisons are impossible because one person cannot know enough about another person's "inner state" of satisfaction or pleasure to be able to compare it quantitatively with his own.[2] There are two serious problems with this reason for concluding that interpersonal utility comparisons cannot be made. First, it assumes an excessively narrow conception of satisfaction (or pleasure or utility)—one which identifies it as a psychological state and, more particularly, an affective state of awareness or feeling.[3] Although it is no doubt true that the terms 'pleasure' and 'satisfaction' are sometimes used to refer to such a state of awareness, we also often speak of *activities* (such as playing tennis or producing a painting) as pleasurable or satisfying even if they are not accompanied by a particular feeling or psychological state of pleasure or satisfaction that is distinct from the activity itself.

More important, this first argument for the impossibility of interpersonal utility comparisons rests upon a now-discredited philosophy of mind which assumes that one can only know of the existence or character of a mental state by introspection (or by "direct" acquaintance). Since one can only introspect one's own mental states, it follows that no one can know of the existence or character of anyone else's mental states of any kind, not just states of pleasure or satisfaction. However, once a broader view of knowledge is adopted, and the assumption that mental states are known only by introspection is abandoned, this first argument for the impossibility of interpersonal utility comparisons loses its force. In particular, it can be argued that an adequate justification for belief in the existence of mental states is the fact that postulating their existence is required for developing the best explanation of certain behavior. On this account, talk about mental states—and claims to knowledge of them—are warranted by their explanatory power, within the context of a theory.

The second argument for the conclusion that interpersonal utility comparisons cannot be made is that there is no nonarbitrary way of selecting a common zero point or baseline from which different individuals' utilities could all be measured and no nonarbitrary way of determining a common unit of measurement. Even if a utility scale can be constructed for each individual by recording the choices made among various goods or options, observation of different individuals' revealed preferences provides no basis for relating their respective utility scales to one another. This second difficulty, unlike the first, depends neither upon an unduly narrow conception of utility as a mental state nor upon the dubious epistemological view that mental states are radically private.

Against this background, the two Paretian principles (that is, Pareto Optimality and Pareto Superiority) are usually seen as second-best alternatives to utilitarianism, the assumption being that assessing social states according to the overall utility they produce would be preferable, were it not for the unfortunate fact that interpersonal utility comparisons cannot be made. The Paretian principles avoid interpersonal utility comparisons by requiring only that we be able to determine whether each individual is better off or worse off relative to *his own* former condition.

Closer examination of this rationale for understanding efficiency according to the Paretian principles quickly dispels the illusion that the choice of a concept of efficiency for evaluating social states is morally neutral. Even if interpersonal utility comparisons could be made accurately, identifying the efficiency of a social state with its tendency to maximize overall utility presupposes a morally controversial view of what a society is. This point can best be appreciated if we recall what is probably the most common, nontechnical notion of efficiency: that of an individual's taking the least costly, effective means to achieving some particular end. The concept of efficiency as overall utility maximization involves a twofold extension of the commonsense notion of efficiency. First, it assumes that the utility of all particular ends can be aggregated into the abstraction of a "total social product" or "overall utility."[4] Second, it assumes that comparing social states according to their tendencies to maximize this abstract "superend" is an appropriate basis for making practical, action-guiding judgments about how society should be organized.

Even if the problem of interpersonal utility comparisons did not cast grave doubts upon the first assumption, the second is itself morally controversial, for the second assumption implies that, for purposes of practical evaluation, society is to be viewed as an apparatus for maximizing overall utility. This view of society may be incompatible with according proper respect to individual persons, who ought not to be regarded merely as contributors to ends that are not their own, including the end of maximizing overall utility. The notion of efficiency as using the least-costly, effective means toward one's own end is not liable to this charge because it assumes unity of purpose, abstracts from conflicts of interest, and does not involve using the individual to achieve ends that are not his own.

Use of the (overall) Utility Maximization Principle, or more simply the Principle of Utility, is also morally controversial because it seems to disregard the intuitively plausible notion that society is or should be, in some basic sense, a *mutually advantageous* arrangement. It is at least possible that maximizing overall utility might permit or even require that one segment of a society should lead the lives of impoverished slaves, so long as the contributions their servitude made to the utility of their masters exceeded the slaves' own disutility. A similar charge can be raised against the assumption that the Pareto Optimality Principle is by itself an appropriate tool for the practical assessment of social arrangements. A situation in which most have nothing and a few have everything may in fact be Pareto Optimal, since improving the condition of the unfortunate majority may require worsening the condition of the privileged minority. A social state may be Pareto Optimal, then, without being mutually advantageous in any sense. This is not surprising since Pareto Optimality focuses only upon the satisfaction of preferences: it is blind to other features that are generally held to be morally relevant, such as the morality or immorality of the preferences themselves and the morality or immorality of the process by which a Pareto Optimal state arose. So, since a social system may satisfy the Pareto Optimality Principle and yet be grossly unfair or unjust, the Pareto Optimality Principle does not by itself provide a sufficient standard for evaluation. The most that can be said is that a system that satisfies the Pareto Optimality Principle is one which has not failed to realize an opportunity for mutual advantage, since a state is Pareto Optimal if and only if there is no feasible state that is Pareto Superior to it.

The Pareto Superiority Principle fares no better in this regard. A move from a Pareto Inferior to a Pareto Superior state may not benefit everyone. The most that can be said is that this move is advantageous for some and at least not disadvantageous to anyone.

Here it is tempting to conclude that *of course* we ought to choose (1) a state in which someone can be made better off without making anyone worse off over (2) a state in which no one can be made better off without making someone worse off. After all, if we make the move from a Pareto Inferior to a Pareto Superior state, *how could anyone have anything to complain about?* So, quite independently of its avoidance of interpersonal utility comparisons, the Pareto Superiority Principle is attractive because it appears to be morally uncontroversial.

However, the claim that no one has grounds for complaining about a change which makes some better off while making none worse off is itself morally controversial. According to some moral theories, and commonsense moral views as well, even a person who benefits from such a change may have grounds for complaint—if, for example, the change was imposed by others without his consent.[5]

In cases of paternalism one individual or group interferes with someone's liberty or opportunities for choice in order to benefit that person. But even cases of successful paternalistic intervention can provoke legitimate complaints from the one who is interfered with. So the mere fact that a change would benefit some without worsening the condition of anyone else does not by itself show that no one has grounds for complaint. Consequently, one cannot argue that the Pareto Superiority Principle is morally uncontroversial because the move to a Pareto Superior state never gives anyone reason for complaint.

The fact that even successful paternalism may be morally controversial is only one instance of a much more general objection to the assumption that the Pareto Superiority Principle is morally uncontroversial. Any moral view which acknowledges that observing valid moral principles may not maximize an individual's interests allows for the possibility that a state may be Pareto Superior but morally inferior. Keeping one's promises, for example, sometimes requires one to forgo advantages that could be reaped by breaking them.

My suggestion, then, is that the strongest case for using the Paretian principles as criteria for assessing the efficiency of social states is not that they are second-best substitutes for utilitarian comparisons, nor that they are morally neutral or even morally uncontroversial. In the absence of agreement on a moral theory, the best that can be said about the Paretian principles is that (1) both bear a remote resemblance to the commonsense notion of efficiency as taking the least-costly effective means to one's particular end; and (2) the Pareto principles approximate the principle that social arrangements should be mutually advantageous in the sense that the attempt to achieve a Pareto Optimal state and the choice of a Pareto Superior state over a Pareto Inferior state both acknowledge that advantages for some are to be gained if this can be done without disadvantaging others. However, the Paretian principles are morally uncontroversial only if they are treated as principles for *prima facie* evaluations of social states, subject to the possibility of countervailing moral evaluations. So even if the Paretian principles are not themselves moral principles and hence even if we can roughly distinguish between arguments based on grounds of efficiency and those based on moral grounds, the decision of how much weight is to be given to the fact that a particular social arrangement satisfies one of these efficiency criteria is not a morally neutral decision.

Economists usually treat the previous definitions of Pareto Optimality and Pareto Superiority as if they were equivalent, respectively, to the following formulations, expressed in terms of individuals' *preferences* rather than in terms of being *better* or *worse off*:

1. *A state, S^1, is Pareto Optimal if and only if there is no feasible alternative state, S^2, such that at least one person prefers S^2 to S^1 and such that no one prefers S^1 to S^2.*
2. *A state, S^1, is Pareto Superior to a state, S^2, if and only if at least one person prefers S^1 to S^2 and no one prefers S^2 to S^1.*

The thesis that the two different formulations are equivalent can be understood in either of two ways: either as a claim about the meaning of the term 'well-being,' namely, that a person's well-being simply is the satisfaction of his preferences; or as the empirical hypothesis that in general a person's own preferences are the most reliable indicator of what will contribute to his well-being. Later, we shall challenge the equivalence thesis when we examine the role which it plays in efficiency arguments for the market, but for now let us assume its correctness.

If the equivalence thesis (on either of its interpretations) is correct, then it may be objected that the Paretian principles *can* take into account moral values in such a way that conflicts between efficiency assessments and moral assessments cannot occur. And if this is so, then contrary to our earlier conclusion, using the Paretian principles as decisive criteria for assessing social arrangements begs no moral questions. According to this argument, an individual's moral values are to be understood simply as very weighty preferences. But if this is the case and if satisfying an individual's preferences makes him better off, then a state, S^1, that is Pareto Superior to another state, S^2, must also be *morally superior* to it. Suppose that S^1 is Pareto Superior to S^2. If S^1 was not consonant with everyone's moral values, but S^2 was, then someone would prefer S^2 to S^1, and therefore (granted the equivalence thesis) someone would be worse off in S^1 than in S^2 (because his moral preferences, to which he gives top priority, would not be satisfied). And if someone would be worse off in S^1 than in S^2, then S^1 would not be Pareto Superior to S^2. But if, by our hypothesis, S^1 *is* Pareto Superior to S^2, then no one is worse off in S^1 than in S^2 and at least one person is better off in S^1 than in S^2. Therefore, if S^1 is Pareto Superior to S^2, then S^1 is morally superior to S^2 (or at least not Pareto Inferior to S^2) as well. So there can be no conflict between Paretian efficiency and morality.

Nevertheless, as I suggested earlier, many, if not most, moral theories, as well as commonsense views of morality, allow for the possibility that what is morally required may not be in the individual's best interest. Indeed, this is something of an understatement, since both moral theories and commonsense discussions of morality emphasize not only conflicts between paternalism and individual autonomy, but also conflicts between self-interest and morality. But if any such conflicts are possible—and surely they are—then either the equivalence thesis is true, that is, satisfying an individual's preferences makes him better off, but moral values are not simply top priority preferences; or moral values are simply top priority preferences, but the equivalence thesis is false, that is, satisfying a person's preferences (in this case his "moral preferences") need not make him better off. Since the argument that efficiency and morality cannot conflict requires the truth of both the equivalence thesis and the thesis that moral values are simply top priority preferences, that argument fails. The problem of weighing moral evaluations against efficiency evaluations cannot be evaded.

Yet another defense of the practice of relying on the Pareto Superiority Principle is the thesis that it is simply a principle of *rationality*: rational individuals necessarily consent to a Pareto improvement, that is, to a move to a Pareto Superior state. Since some gain and none loses, to fail to consent would be to exhibit irrational envy. If the thesis that the Pareto Superiority Principle is a principle of rationality is accepted, the preceding argument that the pursuit of Pareto improvements and the dictates of morality may diverge takes on quite a different significance. For now the advocate of the Pareto Superiority Principle may concede that some may withhold consent from Pareto improvements on moral grounds, but then conclude that such moral scruples are irrational.

As Russell Hardin has argued, however, it is a mistake to hold that the Pareto Superiority Principle is a principle of rationality. Hardin has shown that rational individuals will *not* always consent to Pareto improvements. Instead, they may withhold consent out of rational, *strategic* considerations. Hardin has in mind cases in which it is reasonable to believe that there may be a series of moves in which one's subsequent gains will depend upon the gains others make in earlier moves in the series. Suppose that in move M^1, from S^1 to S^2, A will gain but B will neither gain nor lose. If the potential gains which B can make from subsequent moves (M^2, M^3, and so forth) will be lessened due to the fact that B did not gain in M^1 while A did, then the rational strategy for B may be to refuse to consent to M^1. But if this is so, then the Pareto Superiority Principle is not a principle of rationality per se, but at most a principle which rational individuals would rely on in those circumstances in which different parties' potential gains are not interdependent in ways which make strategic behavior rational.[6]

In the discussion that follows I will examine arguments for and against the market on grounds of (Paretian) efficiency, while for the most part bracketing the difficult question of how much weight considerations of efficiency should be given relative to moral arguments when the two conflict. One suspects that the rather unreflective popularity of the Paretian concept of efficiency is due either to the failure of its adherents to recognize that the Principle of Utility, for which they view the Paretian Principles as a substitute, is not morally neutral, or to their tacit skepticism about the possibility of gaining a consensus on moral theory, or to the mistaken belief that morality and efficiency cannot conflict, or to the equally mistaken belief that the Paretian principles are principles of rationality. A final possibility is that those who rely upon the Paretian concept of efficiency as the sole or primary tool for evaluating economic systems do so because they assume that Utilitarianism is the correct moral theory. But this assumption, as we shall see, is also dubious.

2

Efficiency Arguments For and Against the Market

Efficiency Arguments For *the Market*

The Ideal Market The case for the market on grounds of efficiency rests on two main claims: (1) a theoretical statement that exchanges in the ideal market reach an equilibrium state that is Pareto Optimal (that is, the First Fundamental Theorem of Welfare Economics), and (2) the assumption that actual (nonideal) markets, or feasible modifications of actual markets, sufficiently approximate the efficiency of the ideal market to make them preferable to nonmarket arrangements. We must begin, then, with a description of the conditions that define the ideal market and that ensure that exchanges result in a Pareto Optimal equilibrium state.

1. Full information is available about the performance and quality of goods and services and the costs of all alternative ways of producing them, and the cost of this information is zero.

2. Costs of enforcing contracts and property rights are zero, and property rights, including rights to the means of production, are established and stable.

3. Individuals are rational in this sense: their preferences are organized in a transitive ordering (such that if an individual prefers A to B and B to C, he also prefers A to C) and they are capable of selecting appropriate means toward their ends.

4. (a) Transaction costs are zero (transaction costs include costs of bringing goods and services together for exchange, and costs of reaching agreements for exchange, for example, costs of formulating mutually acceptable contracts, and costs of information about potential offers to buy and sell) *or* (b) there is perfect competition (that is, no

buyer or seller can influence prices by his own independent actions and there is complete freedom to enter and exit the market) and no externalities are present. (An externality is a "neighborhood" or "third-party" effect of a market exchange: an effect on some one's well-being which is not taken into account in the market exchange. Those neighborhood effects which are beneficial are called external economies or positive externalities; those which are detrimental are called external diseconomies or negative externalities. An example of a positive externality is the pleasant view I enjoy of my neighbor's flower garden. The exchange between my neighbor and his landscaper took into account only the costs and benefits to the parties to the exchange, not the benefits to me. An example of a negative externality is a chemical producer's discharge of noxious gases into the air: the cost of breathing bad air is not taken into account in the bargain that is struck between the chemical producer and the customer who buys his product.)

5.   Products offered in the market are undifferentiated—buyers cannot distinguish between the products offered by various sellers, and vice versa.

Pareto Optimal outcomes are guaranteed only if all of these conditions are satisfied. When they are satisfied, production and exchanges will occur until an equilibrium state is reached which is such that no one could be made better off without someone being made worse off.[1]

Since the immensely strong conditions that define the ideal market are never met in actual markets, the case for the market on grounds of efficiency depends on the extent to which actual markets do approximate, or can be modified to approximate, the ideal market.

The Diachronic Efficiencies of the Market   The preceding way of understanding the efficiency of the ideal market, by focusing only on the exchange of existing goods and services, overlooks what may be called the diachronic efficiencies of the market. The latter are efficiencies that result from competition over time. Competition among producers reduces costs of production, since producers who fail to develop and utilize less-costly methods of production are replaced by those who do. Competition among entrepreneurs reduces transaction costs, because the entrepreneur who can match buyers with sellers with the least expenditure of his own resources can charge less for his services and capture a larger share of the market. Finally, the need for information on the part of producers, consumers, and entrepreneurs creates a market for information. In each of these respects, competition in nonideal markets generates incentives for behavior that tends toward the more perfect satisfaction of the conditions of the ideal market, in particular, zero transaction costs, full information, and zero information costs.

Some celebrants of the market, especially F. A. Hayek, have emphasized not only that competition in nonideal markets tends toward more perfect fulfillment of the conditions of the ideal market by efficiently producing and distributing new information, but also that there is a more basic sense in which markets utilize information efficiently.[2] In the market enormous amounts of complex information are utilized in the emergence and adjustments of prices over time, and yet it is not necessary that all of this information, or even a minuscule fraction of it, be possessed by any individual or group for the system to tend toward efficient outcomes. The market thus enables individuals and groups to economize on information.

Hayek's point can best be appreciated if we contrast the information requirements of decentralized allocations production and distribution in the market with the information requirements of attempts to organize a large-scale economy through centralized planning without the aid of markets. Consider, for the purposes of simplicity, only the amount and complexity of information that would have to be gathered and successfully integrated in order to make even a rather limited decision to allocate social resources among alternative lines of production. In order to make a reasonable choice among different proposals for allocating resources across existing and possible lines of production, the individual planner (or planning group) must be able to estimate reliably the costs of producing X amount of good G, relative to Y amount of good H, and so forth for all of the types of goods under consideration. To make such estimates it is necessary for the individual (or group) to integrate a staggering amount of information concerning the least-costly method of production for each producing unit (for example, each physical plant) in each line of production (for example, manufacturing vehicles for public transportation). And even if all of this information were available to each planner and even if each planner were able to integrate it successfully in a cost schedule for all of the goods under consideration at any given time, constant revision would be necessary, since the least-costly method of production for any existing or possible product can change with developments in technology, organizational techniques, and discoveries or depletions of minerals and other raw materials.

All of this, however, is a vast simplification. So far we have proceeded as if information about costs of production were not dependent upon information about individuals' preferences. If the planner's selection of an allocation proposal is to take into account the preferences of the individuals for whom the goods are being produced, he must know what those preferences are—which goods each individual wants, in what amounts, and at what cost in foregone opportunities for enjoying other goods or other goods in larger quantities that might have been produced. The problem of information is profoundly exacerbated once the diachronic dimension is recognized: individual preferences change over time.

In comparison, the information required of participants in the market is minimal. The information a successful consumer or producer or entrepreneur must possess is quite narrow. For example, a producer of tables needs to know if he can expect to sell a certain number of tables at a certain price; he need not know how many tables the economy as a whole should produce, or what the ratio should be of tables relative to automobiles. The same competitive forces that give rise to specialization in the production of goods and sevices also produce specialization in the gathering and using of information. Or, perhaps more accurately, specialization in the gathering and utilization of information is just one aspect of specialization in economic roles in the market. In the case of the entrepreneur this is most obvious, since there is a sense in which information (about possible matches between buyers and sellers) is his only business. But in every case exchangers in the market are specialists in limited, concrete information of various sorts.[3] The market, then, can be viewed as a device for efficiently coordinating the actions of many individuals through specialization in the gathering and use of information.

So far we have contrasted the information requirements of the ideal market and economic planning only from a *cognitive* standpoint, but the case for the market on grounds of efficiency in gathering and utilizing information is strengthened if we also focus on the *motivational* aspects of that process. Those who argue for the market on grounds of informational efficiency can contend not only that their system makes more realistic demands on the individual's cognitive abilities, but also that it makes more realistic demands on individual motivation. The same simple motivational assumptions that explain the tendency toward efficient exchanges in general also explain why it is that the individual will be sufficiently motivated to gather, integrate and apply the limited information he needs. Since the individual will bear the costs of failing to gather and utilize needed information, each has an incentive to be well-informed. Those who reject the argument for the market on grounds of informational efficiency must show not only that planners would have the cognitive ability to gather, integrate and apply vast amounts of complex, constantly changing information; they must also provide a theory of motivation to show that the individuals in question would have sufficient incentives to do what they are cognitively equipped to do.

The Productive Efficiency of the Market   Finally, proponents of the market tout its productive efficiency: it enables a society to maximize overall outputs relative to initial overall inputs. While exchange in the ideal market ensures that an economic pie of a given size will be distributed in a Pareto Optimal fashion, competition—by placing resources in the hands of producers who most closely approximate the least-costly methods of production—increases the size of the economic pie.

Some of the earliest advocates of the market, such as Adam Smith and Bernard Mandeville, suggest that the general argument for the market on grounds of productive efficiency can be applied to the particular case of what they regard as a scarce productive resource: altruistic behavior. Their point is that the market does not rely upon altruistic behavior in satisfying human needs and preferences and that in this sense it economizes on the "expenditure" of altruism. There are several assumptions behind this argument. One is that the scarcity of altruistic behavior is a fact about human nature, or as Hume put it, that men are generally only capable of "limited altruism" directed toward a small circle of family and friends. If in fact the sentiment of altruism is by nature severely limited, and tends to lose its practical effectiveness as we attempt to extend it to more distant individuals, then a system that organizes large numbers of individuals without depending upon altruism will not only avoid futile attempts to rely upon altruism to do what it cannot do; it will also "free up" our limited resources of altruism for their proper function: the effective expression of concern for those with whom we are most closely associated. In this sense, then, the market system uses altruism more efficiently than alternative systems, just as attaching a button with a thread is a more efficient use of that thread than attempting to use it to hoist a boulder.[4]

Critics of the market, whether they be romantic conservatives who pine for the alleged altruism of premarket communities or Marxian socialists who predict a widening of altruism in postcapitalist society, challenge this empirical assumption. They argue that the limited altruism which Hume and Smith took for an unalterable feature of the human condition is in fact a transient characteristic of human beings in market society. They conclude that the fact that the market system does not require lavish expenditures of the scarce resource of altruism is hardly an argument for the market system if it produced the "shortage" of altruism in the first place.

Efficiency Arguments **Against** *the Market:*
Major Sources of Inefficiency

The most obvious challenges to the market on grounds of efficiency
are attempts to show that actual market processes fail to satisfy
important conditions of the ideal market. Inefficiencies result from
(a) high transaction costs, (b) lack of information on the part of
producers and consumers, (c) monopolistic tendencies, (d) the presence
of externalities, (e) the existence of barriers to successful voluntary
collective action to secure certain goods which the market cannot
provide (public goods), (f) lack of congruence between the satisfaction
of the individual's preferences as they are revealed in the market and
the individual's well-being, and (g) unemployment.

High Transaction Costs   Actual markets tend toward Pareto Optimal
outcomes only to the extent that transaction costs approximate the
zero transaction costs of the ideal market. But transaction costs are
never zero in the real world. Buyers and sellers must struggle with
various logistical problems, including those involving transportation
and communication costs. Strategic behavior (for example, bluffing
with lower offers than one is prepared to pay or threatening to
withdraw from the bargaining process) are also transaction costs.
Further, if the total costs of the legal system as far as it is involved
with the drafting, interpretation, and enforcement of contracts is
included, transaction costs are enormous. The most that can be said
in defense of actual markets here is that competition tends to reduce
transaction costs.

Lack of Information   A host of psychological, institutional, and tech-
nological factors ensure that producers and consumers in actual markets
lack information required for Pareto Optimal outcomes. Producers
must proceed on the basis of often highly speculative predictions of
changing consumer preferences, and even experienced firms may
overproduce or underproduce. Producers also often lack information
about the methods of production employed by rival firms, either
because producers with less-costly methods deliberately keep this
information secret, or because it is restricted by patents, or because
it is too costly to obtain, or because it is simply overlooked. (The
primary information-gathering task is the gathering of information
about what sort of information to look for and where to look for it.)
Similarly, consumers may lack relevant information about the existence
of alternative products or about the quality or performance of products.

Lack of consumer information about medical care is often cited as an example of ignorance as a barrier to efficient outcomes in the market. Defenders of the market reply that consumer ignorance here is largely a result of lack of competition among producers because of licensure laws which limit competition by restricting entry into the market and because of laws and professional codes of ethics which prohibit or discourage advertising. It is extremely difficult, however, to determine to what extent the removal of these sorts of barriers to competition would in fact remedy the deficiency of consumer information, since the technical character of some information may itself be an obstacle to consumers.

While the defender of the market relies upon advertising, broadly construed, and competition to ameliorate deficiencies of information, the critic of the market counters by pointing out that successful advertising often consists at least in part of nonrational appeals which either misrepresent, or omit altogether, relevant information. Further, attempts to ameliorate this problem by monitoring advertising in order to enforce prohibitions against misrepresentation may be extremely costly and relatively ineffective. And even in cases in which there is no misrepresentation, advertising may stimulate demand without conveying information which the individual himself, upon considered judgment, would agree is relevant to the making of a reasonable choice, granted his own stable preferences.

Monopolistic Tendencies Monopolistic tendencies exist when some exchanger can unilaterally influence prices. We have already seen several circumstances which make this possible: restrictions on entry into markets due to licensure, prohibitions against advertising, and trade secrets. Monopolistic tendencies may also result, of course, from government support (as in the case of legal prohibitions against the delivery of first-class mail by anyone other than the U.S. Post Office) or from collusion among firms to fix prices or drive out competitors or by some combination of government support and collusion. In principle, at least, so-called natural monopolies can arise and persist without government support if some firms happen to enjoy unique access to certain raw materials or if economies of scale make it difficult for new firms to survive long enough to amass sufficient capital to produce competitively.

There is, however, considerable dispute as to whether "natural" and collusive monopolies pose a serious threat to efficiency in the absence of government support. It can be argued that both "natural" and collusive monopolies are inherently unstable and tend to break down eventually through competition. Advocates of the market often infer, then, that government-supported monopoly is the only serious threat to efficiency in the long run. They then go on to draw the *additional* conclusion that monopolistic inefficiencies are not a serious objection to the market because they arise only when the market is not allowed to operate freely. This last conclusion, however, is a gross non sequitur. Even if monopolies would vanish or be of little consequence if they were not supported by government, it would follow that the presence of monopolies is not a serious objection to the market on grounds of efficiency *only if* there were good reason to believe that government support for monopolies can *in fact* be eliminated. It would be an error of excessive rationalism to assume that once it is recognized that monopolies reduce overall efficiency, firms and government officials will cease the practice of government support for monopolies.

Several prominent political economists have recently attempted to extend the scope of market explanations to account for the phenomenon of government regulation of the market, including government regulation that serves to support monopolies. According to one theory of regulation, government regulators provide a service (regulation which serves to limit competition) to firms which "pay" for the services, not exclusively or even primarily by outright bribes or campaign contributions, but by supporting publicly financed bureaucratic positions which include compensation not only in the form of salaries, pensions, and health benefits, but also perquisites of various sorts.[5] A closely related and compatible theory purports to explain bureaucratic behavior, including regulation in support of monopolies, on the basis of a very small number of behavioral axioms, the most important of which is that bureaucrats tend to act so as to maximize the "budget" of their bureau—where the "budget" includes not only salaries but also fringe benefits, perquisites, and so forth.[6] Whether or not these or rival theories are in fact correct, the crucial point is that those who attempt to rebut criticisms of the market by showing that all significant monopolies depend upon government intervention and would not occur in a "free" market owe us an explanation of the pervasive phenomenon of government-supported monopoly. And more importantly, the explanation they provide must show that the removal of government support, and hence the increased efficiency that depends upon it, is a politically feasible goal, if their defense of the market is to have practical force.

Externalities Critics of the market have been quick to point out the pervasiveness and seriousness of neighborhood effects, or externalities, as a key source of the market's failure to achieve efficient outcomes. Perhaps the most commonly cited contemporary example is the external costs that are imposed on people who breathe air polluted by chemical producers. Such negative externalities can be viewed as inefficiencies of *overproduction*. More of the chemical is produced than would be produced if the total costs of production, including the costs to breathers of polluted air, were taken into account in establishing the equilibrium price for the product. Because the cost to the producer of producing the chemical is less than it would be if the costs to third parties were included in his costs, the producer can sell the chemical at a lower price and still make a profit. But since more will be sold at this lower price, more will be produced than would be if the total costs, including detrimental third-party effects, were taken into account.

Positive externalities (beneficial third-party effects) are also inefficient. Standard examples include the beneficial effects of education and vaccination. It is argued that private exchanges for educational services, at least the more basic ones, generate beneficial effects for those not involved in the exchange. (An educated citizenry is valuable to society at large, not simply to those who purchase educational services or to those who are paid to provide them.) Similarly, if some individuals purchase vaccinations, others who do not will benefit from this exchange because the probability of contracting the disease in question will decrease for everyone, including those who are not vaccinated. Positive externalities, then, can be viewed as inefficiencies of *underproduction:* if the benefits of something can be had without purchasing it, then less of it will be produced (if any of it is produced at all) than would be produced if all the benefits flowing from it were obtainable only through purchase.

Failure to Provide Public Goods   Anticipation of positive externalities can result in the failure to provide *public goods*.[7] There are five features of public goods which together can result in a failure to provide the good: (a) Action by some or all members of the group is necessary and sufficient to provide the good, but action by one or a few members is not sufficient. (b) The good, if provided, will be available to all, including noncontributors (jointness of supply). (c) There is no way or no practical way to prevent noncontributors from partaking of the good (nonexcludability). (d) The individual's contribution is a cost to that individual. In the case of a *pure* public good, there is an additional feature: (e) One individual's consumption of the good does not diminish the supply of it available to others.

Two related problems can prevent the provision of a good when conditions a–d are satisfied. One, the *free-rider problem* occurs when some or all individuals attempt to take a free ride on the presumed contributions of others to the provision of the good in question. The individual, if rational, will conclude that either enough others will contribute to achieve the good, in which case his contribution (which is a cost to him) would be wasted; or not enough others will contribute to achieve the good, in which case his contribution (which is a cost to him) would again be wasted. Since the individual's contribution is a cost to him, he will, if rational, conclude that regardless of whether or not others contribute, he should not contribute. But if all or a sufficient number of individuals reason thusly, the good will not be provided.

The second barrier to successful collective action is the *assurance problem*. An individual who is willing to contribute if assured that others will contribute, does not intend to take a free ride on the efforts of others. Nevertheless, if he has reason to believe that others will not contribute (perhaps because *they* will attempt to be free-riders), he may decide not to contribute.

Attempts to use strictly voluntary agreements to eliminate either negative externalities, as in the case of chemical pollution, or positive externalities, as in the case of public goods such as national defense or the benefits of having an educated citizenry or of vaccination, can be blocked by the free-rider and assurance problems. For example, if several polluting chemical firms make a purely voluntary, unenforced agreement to limit or eliminate the discharge of air-borne pollutants, each firm will have an incentive for noncompliance: they may not comply, either in order to take a free ride on the compliance of others, or because of lack of assurance that others will comply, or both. While either the free-rider or assurance problems may by itself be sufficient to block collective action, competition ensures that the free-rider problem will be the dominant difficulty. A firm which complies only on the condition of assurance that others will do so will at least avoid being placed at a competitive disadvantage relative to others. But even if a particular firm has assurance that all others will comply it would gain a competitive advantage over others by taking a free ride and not complying. Similarly, a purely voluntary, unenforced agreement to contribute to the provision of national defense or to participate in a vaccination program may also break down either because some attempt to take a free ride and reap an external benefit from the "exchange" among those who do comply or because they are unwilling to comply unless they are assured that others will keep their part of the bargain of exchanging compliance for compliance.

Government may intervene in the market in several ways to attempt to eliminate externalities or to overcome public goods problems.

1. Government officials may attempt to persuade parties who are producing negative externalities such as pollution, to comply voluntarily with an announced program or to conform voluntarily to an announced standard. Such efforts, however, are vulnerable to the assurance and free-rider problems and are unlikely to succeed.

2. Government may simply prohibit the behavior that produces the negative externality (for example, outlaw the manufacture of the polluting substance). This alternative may itself be inefficient if there is no pollution-free way to produce the product and if the product is highly valued.

3. Government may allow the activity that produces the negative externality to continue, but tax the producer either in order to reduce the volume of production by increasing production costs or in order to use the tax-proceeds to compensate those who suffer the ill effects of the activity, or both.

4. Government may set and enforce standards which those engaged in the activity must meet (for example, clean air standards for industrial smokestacks).

5. Government may enforce a legal system which allows affected third parties (either individually or in class-actions) to sue for compensation for costs imposed on them by the actions of others.[8]

6. Government may enforce voluntary agreements among individuals or groups.

7. Government may create and enforce private property rights in order to "internalize" externalities or "privatize" public goods—that is, to transform a public good into a collection of privately consumable goods for which the free-rider problem does not arise. For example, if the free-rider problem vitiates voluntary agreements to avoid overgrazing of communal pastures or open range or to limit fur-trapping or lumbering in national forests, government may create private property rights to the resources in question.[9] At least in the case of such replenishable natural resources, private ownership provides individuals with incentives to conserve which are not present in situations in which resources are unowned or communally owned. In many cases, however, externalities cannot be internalized and public goods cannot be privatized because private property rights in the item in question are not feasible. For example, the problem of preventing acid rain (an externality) or of obtaining clean air (a public good) cannot be solved in this way because private property rights in the planet's atmosphere are not feasible.

8. Government itself may become the provider of a public good which the market fails to provide because of the assurance or free-rider problems. Perhaps the most commonly cited example is government provision of city parks, the idea being that since noncontributors could benefit from these pleasant environments they would probably not come about through voluntary contribution schemes or through private market exchanges.

The inability of the market to eliminate externalities and to provide public goods is a serious and pervasive departure from efficiency. However, if this is to serve as a sufficient reason either for attempting to abandon the market altogether or for restricting its scope by government intervention or by supplementing it with government provision of goods and services, additional premises are needed. First, it must be shown that government intervention, government provision of goods and services, or some other alternative to the market, will itself be less costly—that is, will not involve equally great or greater inefficiences than the market.

This crucial assessment becomes more difficult to support once it is understood that governmental intervention may itself produce externalities, and that limiting government intervention may itself be a public good, subject to the free-rider and assurance problems. Government regulation—especially because it is devised and administered by fallible human beings—may hinder innovation, contribute to inflation and unemployment by raising production costs, and endanger civil and political liberties by concentrating too much power in the government. Excessive generosity in the awarding of compensation to those adversely affected by externalities may also contribute to higher prices. Although each individual may recognize that the cumulative effects of singly salutory government interventions in the market may make us all worse off, the individual may nonetheless find it rational to refrain from exercising restraint when it comes to those particular interventions which promise to advance his own goals or those interventions which, considered in isolation, may benefit all. To assume that if each member of a set of interventions is by itself compatible with the continued well-functioning of the market, then the whole set is similarly compatible, is to commit the fallacy of composition. (From the fact that each grain of sand in a mountain of sand is light it does not follow that the mountain is light.) Moreover, since the public good in question is the limitation of government activity, the standard response to difficulties in achieving public goods— recourse to government intervention to solve the assurance and free-rider problems—can hardly be expected to work.

More radical critics of the market might protest at this point that the need to show that inefficiencies due to government intervention in the market would not equal or exceed the inefficiencies they are designed to eliminate is a serious problem only if one proposes to reform rather than *abolish* the market system. The problem of weighing these government inefficiencies does not arise for more fundamental proposals to replace the market with an alternative system. The fact that intervening in inefficient market processes may produce equally worrisome inefficiencies may be a sign that the whole system should be scrapped, not a vindication of a noninterventionist policy.

If this radical challenge to the market on grounds of efficiency is to have force, however, *the alternative system must be explained in sufficient detail to make efficiency comparisons between it and the market system possible.* The argument would then have to be that the alternative system would provide a closer approximation to the efficiency of the ideal market than the nonideal market system we now have or are likely to have through modifying the current system.

In the next section I shall explore some profound obstacles to making any such *intersystemic efficiency comparisons*—whether in favor of the market system or in favor of an alternative system. For the present it will suffice to note that there is a basic sense in which all of the efficiency arguments for the market and all attempts to rebut them by pointing out the failure of actual markets to satisfy the conditions of the ideal market are essentially incomplete, unless they include support for such comparison. Arguments in favor of actual markets on the basis of the claim that they approximate the efficiency of the ideal market are conclusive only if they give us good reason to believe that actual markets approximate (or can be made to approximate) the outcomes of the ideal market *more* closely than feasible nonmarket systems would. Similarly, merely showing that actual markets do not achieve the efficiency of the ideal market does not establish that greater efficiency can be gained either by further regulating or reducing the scope of existing markets or by replacing the entire market system with an alternative.

Lack of Congruence Between Individual Well-being and the Satisfaction of Preferences Revealed in the Market   It was observed earlier that another fundamental condition for efficiency in the ideal competitive market is the assumption that satisfying an individual's preferences, as the latter are revealed in his exchanges in the market, makes him better off. And as was also noted, this assumption can be understood either as resting on the claim that 'well-being' simply means satisfaction of revealed preferences or upon the empirical claim that in general the preferences an individual reveals in his market behavior are the most reliable indicator of what will in fact make him better off. As a meaning claim, the assumption must be rejected. It makes perfectly good sense to ask whether satisfying a particular preference in fact makes one better off. One reason why this is so is that, at least in the less than perfect conditions of actual markets, individuals can be and are mistaken about what is most conducive to their own good, either because they are less than perfectly knowledgeable or less than perfectly rational, or both. The empirical version of the assumption is more plausible, but far from uncontroversial.

Perhaps the most potentially serious criticism of the empirical version of the assumption and hence of the efficiency argument for the market which relies upon it, is the Marxist objection that the market process itself tends to generate "distorted" preferences whose satisfaction does not promote the individual's well-being.[10] Hence even if the market does a good job of satisfying the preferences people express in it, outcomes will not be efficient according to that formulation of the Pareto Optimality Principle which focuses on well-being.

Here I will consider only one especially serious attempt to fill out this Marxist objection. G.A. Cohen has argued that advanced capitalism produces a lack of congruence between well-being and the satisfaction of preferences expressed in the market because it has a tendency toward expanding output and consumption at the expense of reducing toil.[11] Like Marx, Cohen acknowledges that capitalism greatly increases productivity—that the ratio of outputs to inputs is much greater in capitalism than in premarket modes of production, such as feudalism. Increased productivity provides an opportunity either to reduce toil (roughly, unwanted labor activity), while maintaining the same level of output; or to expand output, without reducing toil; or to strike some balance between reduced toil and expanded output.

However, Cohen argues, the same competitive self-interest that results in greater productivity produces a bias toward continual expansion of outputs and toward encouraging (through advertising) continually increasing consumption of what is produced. Now at some point, increased freedom from toil (that is, leisure) is rationally preferable to increased consumption. Advanced capitalism is irrational (or, as an economist would say, inefficient) because it has an inherent tendency to push output and consumption past the optimal trade-off point between leisure and toil.

This argument, however, is far from convincing. First of all, at most it establishes that advanced capitalism has a *tendency* toward irrationality. It does not rule out the possibility that this tendency will be held in check by opposing tendencies.[12] Two obvious opposing tendencies are competition for labor and labor union activity. Labor unions can and do fight for shorter working hours and more pleasant work environments. And, if firms must compete for labor, one way to attract employees is to offer less toilsome work, either by shortening working hours or by making work more intrinsically rewarding. Further, even if firms do not advertise directly for increased leisure (they do not, as Cohen notes, explicitly encourage us to forgo consumption to have more leisure time), nonetheless, advertisements for leisure products and services may indirectly encourage people to increase leisure time if only by leading them to reflect upon whether their current patterns of consumption permit them to take advantage of desirable leisure products and services. For example, if I see an advertisement for golf clubs or for fishing rods which persuasively portrays the pleasures of outdoor sports, I may be prompted to reconsider my decision to take a higher-paying but more time-consuming job which would not permit me to engage in these recreational activities.

Furthermore, it can be argued that even if advanced capitalism has a tendency toward inefficient trade-offs between leisure and toil, this tendency is not unique to capitalism. There is considerable empirical evidence to suggest that Soviet planners continue to expand output at the expense of individual well-being in order to support a massive military establishment both at home and in client countries and in order to compete in a "growth race" with the United States and other nonsocialist countries such as West Germany.

Cohen attempts to counter this objection by arguing that while the tendency toward overexpansion of output is an *inherent* feature of the market *economy*, it is only the result of defective *political arrangements* in socialist countries.[13] This is an odd reply for a Marxist to make, however, for several reasons. First, it is distinctive of Marxist social theory to deny the autonomy of the political realm from the economic realm, but Cohen's reply assumes that a sharp distinction can be made between the Soviet economy and Soviet political policy. This is an especially difficult distinction to make in a "command economy," in which the commands emanate from the political hierarchy. Further, Cohen's assumption that captialism's tendency toward overexpansion will *not* be held in check assumes that the political process in capitalism will not be able to put a brake on the tendency because the political realm is dominated by the economic realm. Yet he gives us no good reasons to think that policy choices will stem overexpansion in socialism but will not do so in capitalism.

The Marxist rejoinder, of course, would be to claim that policy choices in socialism are *more likely* to avoid overexpansion than policy choices in capitalism because in capitalism policy choices are strongly influenced, if not determined by, market interests. This reply, however, is inadequate because it does not explain why the political process in the Soviet Union has failed to check overexpansionist tendencies in spite of the absence of the influence of market interests. What the Marxist needs, but does not at this point possess, is a theory of socialist policy formation capable of showing that success in resisting over-expansionist tendencies is significantly more likely in a socialist system than in a market system.

There is, however, a more fundamental incompleteness in the Marxist objection. That objection assumes that well-being is a function of at least two factors, leisure and consumption of goods and services, and then argues that the market system tends to increase consumption at the expense of leisure. Yet even if it can be shown that this tendency will not be checked in capitalism, the result is a telling argument against the market system *only if there is a feasible alternative system which is also highly productive.* In other words, demonstrating that a nonmarket system would not tend to increase toil beyond the optimal leisure/toil trade-off point is not sufficient to establish the superiority of that system unless that system can be shown at least to approach the productivity of the market system. For if the alternative is suf-ficiently unproductive, the market system may be preferable, on grounds of efficiency, even if the market system fails to achieve the optimal leisure/toil trade-off.

However, it is impossible to show that a feasible nonmarket system at least approaches the productivity of the market unless (1) a rather well-developed theoretical model of the nonmarket system is available, and (2) it is demonstrated that a sufficiently productive approximation of the ideal socialist system described in the theoretical model is practically possible. Unfortunately, neither Cohen nor other contem-porary Marxists, nor Marx himself, has achieved even the first step— that of providing a theoretical model for a nonmarket system—in sufficient detail to support the judgment that even this ideal system would achieve a high level of productivity, while at the same time exhibiting the other desirable characteristics that Marxists attribute to communism.

Marx and most later Marxists, including Cohen, assume not only that a highly productive alternative to the market is feasible, but that a high level of productivity and a system for efficiently distributing what is produced can be achieved by a system of *democratic* decision-making. At least in the dominant Marxist tradition, then, the question of whether the market system should be rejected on grounds of efficiency in favor of a socialist alternative depends upon articulating *a theory of democratic social coordination* whose explanatory power is comparable to that of the ideal market model. Such a theory, if it were available, would have to address a number of well-known arguments against democratic decision-making on grounds of efficiency.

Among the most important sources of inefficiency in democratic decision-making for the allocation of resources and the production and distribution of goods in a large-scale economy are (1) time-costs and (2) information-costs of the procedure itself. In a democratic process, the ever-scarce resource of time is consumed lavishly, first, in articulating issues and presenting an agenda to voters; second, in discussing the issues; and third, in actually achieving a decision (where this may involve rounds of voting). Even if the use of electronic mass-media technology could reduce the first source of time-costs, the second and third may still result in great inefficiency, especially where decisions are interdependent and must be made quickly or in a definite, time-ordered sequence. Time-costs are particularly troublesome where the unanimity rule is used, but they are also present in all other forms of majority rule.

The exorbitant information-costs of democratic procedures are no less grave. For complex, large-scale allocation decisions, information required for a rational decision may not be available or may be available only at great cost, or will often be so complex that it will be very difficult if not impossible for any individual or group of individuals to integrate and apply it. There may also be motivational impediments to the gathering, integration, and application of information. In many cases the individual will reasonably believe that his vote will not be decisive. The individual may then reason that either enough others who share his preferences will vote on a given issue to achieve the outcome he prefers, even if he does not vote; or that not enough others will vote to achieve the outcome he prefers, even if he does vote. Thus he may conclude that regardless of how others vote, the rational thing for him to do is not to vote, since voting (as well as becoming sufficiently informed on the issues) is a cost. This is just to say that informed voter participation is a public good, subject to the free-rider problem.

Further, in many cases the individual will lack an incentive to expend time and resources in order to become informed and to vote simply because the issue in question will be of little consequence to him. We have already seen the enormous amount of ever-shifting information required for making allocation and distribution decisions for a large-scale economy and how little information individuals need in the market system by comparison (see p. 17).

The use of representatives, of policy packages, and of centralization in the process of gathering, integrating, and disseminating information can all be viewed as attempts to reduce the time- and information-costs of democratic decision-making. Pareto Optimal outcomes are hardly likely, however, if the voter must choose a package of policies (some of which he does not endorse) or must rely upon a representative (who will at best vote in accordance with some but not all his preferences). Moreover, centralization of the information process, even if done efficiently, threatens to undermine the *democratic* character of the decision-making process by concentrating power in those who control the data upon which others make their decisions.

But even if we set aside inefficiencies due to time- and information-costs, there is another important source of inefficiency in democratic decision-making. Pareto Suboptimality is a direct consequence of the fact that majority decisions are incapable of taking into account the *intensity* of an individual's preferences. Suppose Jones favors policy *P* very strongly, while Smith opposes *P*, but not strongly. If Jones were able to engage in vote-bargaining—to trade his vote on some other issue about which Smith does care strongly or if Jones were able to give Smith a "side payment" in exchange for Smith's favorable vote on *P*—then both Jones and Smith would be better off than if they simply vote their preferences. Vote-bargaining, either in the form of trading or selling votes, allows individuals to express the intensity of their preferences, while majority rule voting does not. As with representatives, policy packages, and centralization of information, avoiding inefficiency through vote-bargaining comes at a steep price. Vote-bargaining undermines the ideal of equal control that animates the insistence on democratic control over allocation and distribution, because it is equivalent to giving some individuals more votes than others on a given issue by giving them fewer votes on other issues. Vote-bargaining, then, is not a device for achieving efficient democratic social coordination; it is a way of achieving efficiency at the expense of democracy.

Of course the decision to allow vote-bargaining for certain types of decisions might itself be arrived at by some form of democratic, that is, majority, rule. But to admit this is not to deny that vote-bargaining erodes the fundamental commitment to equal control over decisions—it is only to recognize that a procedure which is democratic may be used to undermine its own continued use in the future.

The point of this brief discussion is not to demonstrate that an efficient democratic alternative to the market is impossible, but rather to emphasize that a *theory* of efficient democratic social coordination must be developed to support Marxist criticisms of the market on grounds of efficiency.[14]

Unemployment Critics of the market are quick to point out that the foregoing list of sources of inefficiency is incomplete because it fails to acknowledge the problem of unemployment. Unemployment, as we noted earlier, is an instance of aggregative inefficiency—a failure to utilize all available productive resources, in this case labor power.

The simple economic models used to show that the ideal market system will reach a Pareto Optimal equilibrium state disguise the problem insofar as they *assume* full employment. In other words, when it is demonstrated that production and exchange in the ideal market result in a Pareto Optimal equilibrium it is assumed that everyone whose welfare is taken into account in the statement that "no one can be made better off without making someone worse off" is actually participating as an exchanger and/or producer in the system.

There are two ways to understand the charge that unemployment is a serious inefficiency of the market system. The less radical, but nonetheless important interpretation is that even if the ideal market system would reach an equilibrium in which there is full employment (of all who wish to work), imperfect, real world market systems suffer from grave inefficiencies due to unemployment. The second, more radical interpretation of the charge is that even in the ideal market system there is no guarantee that there will be full employment at equilibrium. Let us consider each of these interpretations in turn.

There is much dispute about what the causes of unemployment are in real world market systems and, where a plurality of causes is acknowledged, disagreement remains concerning the magnitudes of their respective contributions to the problem. Some theorists tend to lay the blame chiefly on government activity (for example, the enforcement of minimum wage laws which make it too costly for some employers to hire less-productive workers) and on restrictions on competition for wages due to successful labor union activities. What is common to these views is that they maintain that unemployment is (at least in the main) not an imperfection of the market but rather a result of failure to allow the market to function without interference. The next conclusion usually drawn in this line of reasoning is that since unemployment would be eliminated or at least greatly reduced if the market were allowed to operate freely, the problem of unemployment does not pose a serious objection to the use of markets on grounds of efficiency (nor, for that matter, on ethical grounds). This conclusion, however, does not follow at all, unless a controversial premise is added, namely that it is in fact, or is likely to become, *politically feasible* to eliminate those interferences with the market which (according to this theory) cause unemployment. At this point we are again confronted with the yawning gap between statements about the efficiency of the ideal market and the justification of actual market systems on grounds of efficiency. The fact that unemployment could be greatly reduced if labor unions were abolished or if government ceased intervening (if it is a fact) is not an adequate defense of the market if it is extremely unlikely that labor unions will be abolished or that government intervention will cease.

Ironically enough, the tendency to overlook this gap may stem from a failure to apply economic models developed to explain market processes to the activity of labor unions and of governments. If one assumes that such activity is essentially arbitrary or is an aberration due to ignorance or to a failure to act rationally, one may be tempted to minimize the problem of eliminating these interferences with the market. On the other hand, if the basic tools for analyzing exchanges are applied successfully to the behavior of individuals engaged in labor union activities and to bureaucrats and legislators responding to various special interest groups (including labor unions), it may turn out that these interventions are the predictable—and stable—results of the rationally self-interested interactions of the individuals in question. As such, they may be extremely difficult to eliminate, without effecting significant structural changes in political as well as economic institutions. Yet the same sort of analysis may show that these very political and economic structures are highly resistant to change.

On the second, more radical interpretation, the object is that even in a perfectly competitive market the equilibrium state need not be a state of full employment. So even if the departures from perfect competition just mentioned could be eliminated, unemployment might still exist.

The mere possibility that a perfectly competitive market equilibrium could coexist with unemployment is not, of course, a telling objection. However, once the reasons for concluding that this possibility exists are understood, the objection can be stated much more strongly as the charge that *there is no reason to believe that full employment will be achieved at equilibrium*, even in a perfectly competitive market.

The radical version of the unemployment objection can best be understood as a criticism of the traditional neoclassical economists' argument to show that even if unemployment did occur at some point, a perfectly competitive system would automatically move to a full-employment equilibrium state, without any need for government intervention. The neoclassical argument, in its simplest form, is as follows. Suppose that at present there is some unemployment. If there is free competition for jobs, then (since the supply of labor relative to the demand for it is high), the price of labor, that is, wages, will decrease. As wages decrease, production costs decrease. In attempting to maximize profits, firms act so as to make the marginal cost of their products (the cost of producing one additional unit of the product) equal to the price of the product. In order to equalize marginal costs and price, firms expand production. But expanding production requires hiring more workers. Therefore unemployment is reduced.

Marx and other early critics of capitalism pointed out a problem which this argument overlooks: the problem of *decreasing aggregate demand*, that is, the total demand for what is produced in the economy. Firms will not expand production if they notice that the additional output is not being bought by consumers. But if wages are sufficiently low and if a large enough portion of the consuming public pays for its assumption through wages, then aggregate demand will be insufficient, expansion of production will not occur, additional workers will not be hired, and unemployment will persist.

The neoclassicists had a reply which seemed to rule out the possibility that expansion would be blocked by deficient aggregate demand. Relying upon the work of the eighteenth-century economist J. B. Say, they noted that since at market equilibrium every good produced generates an equivalent value of income, a shortfall of aggregate demand could not exist at equilibrium. So far as unemployment results from insufficient aggregate demand, then, the market system, if left to function freely, would eventually eliminate unemployment.

This last argument contains a hidden assumption which was challenged by John Maynard Keynes in *The General Theory of Employment, Interest, and Money*. Keynes argued that even if every good produced generates income of equivalent value, the proportion of income saved relative to the proportion invested may vary. But continued expansion of production (and hence the reduction of unemployment) depends upon the proportion of income devoted to investment. Unless enough of the income from what is produced is "plowed back" into production, not enough expansion will occur to overcome the problem of insufficient aggregate demand and unemployment will continue to exist. Keynes concluded that there is no reason to believe that precisely the correct relationship between savings and investment will be achieved at equilibrium to ensure full employment. His proposed *solution* to the problem of unemployment (which should be carefully distinguished from his critique of the neoclassical view) is government intervention in the form of fiscal and monetary policies to stimulate aggregate demand. Though Keynes was concerned with the problem of unemployment in real world market systems, it is important to emphasize that his criticism of the neoclassical argument for full-employment market equilibrium does not depend upon the assumption that˙real world market systems are not perfectly competitive.

The Keynesian solution to the problem of unemployment comes at a price: the risk of trading inefficiency due to unemployment for a more or less general lowering of real income (and hence welfare) due to inflation. Producers will respond to an increase in demand by expanding production, by raising prices, or both. But if the economy is already operating at near productive capacity (so that production cannot readily be increased), the prices will increase significantly.

It is not within the scope of this essay to provide anything like a comprehensive critical survey of the debate over the causes and cures of unemployment or the optimal trade-off between unemployment and inflation. Instead, it is sufficient for our purposes to understand that there are three key points at which these complex debates bear on the assessment of the market on grounds of efficiency. First, the problem of unemployment in the market system can be raised both as a serious criticism of the way in which imperfectly competitive, real world market systems work, and, more radically, as indicating an important weakness in the theory of the efficiency of the perfectly competitive market. Second, even if the more radical argument could be conclusively refuted, and even if it could be established that unemployment is not a market imperfection but rather an artifact of interferences with the market, this would not be enough to show that inefficiency due to unemployment is not a grave problem for actual or politically feasible market systems. Third—and this point rarely emerges in the debate over unemployment—the Keynesian charge that market equilibrium and unemployment can coexist is not limited to *private property* market systems. Nothing in Keynes's argument turns on the fact that the actors in the market are individuals (or heads of households) rather than, say, competing, worker-controlled firms. Instead, the point is that the market in general—not just the market with private property in the means of production—does not guarantee the proper relationship between savings and investment to assure full employment at equilibrium. To this extent, then, if Keynes's attack on the neoclassical assumption of full-employment equilibrium is sound, it provides a rationale for intervention in the market in general, not just the market with private property in the means of production. It does not follow, of course, that the appropriate response to unemployment will be the same in every market system, much less that it will be Keynes's solution.

In order to turn the argument from unemployment into an argument against private property market systems, it would be necessary to do much more than to defend the Keynesian critique against its detractors. It would be necessary to defend a nonmarket system, arguing that such a system would avoid the inefficiency which market systems suffer due to unemployment, without itself falling prey to other, equally serious inefficiencies. Or it would be necessary to argue that a market socialist system would be better able to intervene in the market to ameliorate the problem of unemployment than a private property market system, without incurring other, equally costly inefficiencies. We have already examined some of the difficulties of the first alternative. The chapter on market socialism discusses the second.

The Problem of Comparing Whole Systems

Intersystemic Efficiency Comparisons, from Adam Smith to Karl Marx   We have seen that arguments to show that actual markets fail to achieve the efficiency of the ideal market are essentially incomplete. They provide a conclusive case against the market only if they include a theoretical model powerful enough to support the comparative judgment that a nonmarket alternative system is less inefficient than actual markets. It would be a mistake, however, to assume that only the case *against* the market suffers from incompleteness. There is a sense in which all of the efficiency arguments for the market are also incomplete. Even if it is true that the ideal market (necessarily) achieves Pareto Optimal outcomes and even if actual (nonideal) markets *tend* toward Pareto Optimality, it does not follow that a nonideal market system is preferable on grounds of efficiency to all feasible alternative systems unless all of the feasible alternatives do an even worse job of approximating the Pareto Optimal outcomes of the ideal market.

Some of the most famous advocates of the market (from Adam Smith to Milton Friedman), while acknowledging that actual markets fall short of the efficiency of the ideal market, have advanced *intersystemic efficiency* comparisons—comparisons of the overall efficiency of the (nonideal) market system with the overall efficiency of actual or feasible nonmarket systems. Both John Locke and Adam Smith confidently proclaimed that even a poor person in the market system of the England of their day was better off than the richest and most powerful member of the nonmarket system under which American Indians were thought to live.[15] Contemporary advocates of the market, such as Friedman, also often state or imply that the market system as it is found in the United States is more efficient overall than socialist systems, such as that of the Soviet Union. Remarkably little is said, however, about how these comparisons between systems are to be made. Similarly, socialists from Marx to Gerald Cohen often criticize the inefficiency of the market system, implying that there is a feasible socialist alternative that more closely approximates the ideal of efficiency.

The Barriers to Intersystemic Efficiency Comparisons   Neither side has appreciated the formidable obstacles to making intersystemic efficiency comparisons. The depth of the problem can best be appreciated by examining several alternative proposals for grounding such comparisons and for uncovering their problematic presuppositions.

We noted earlier that there is broad agreement that efficiency is to be understood as Pareto Optimality and that the concept of Pareto Superiority is to be used for making comparative efficiency judgments. However, the Pareto Superiority Principle is designed to permit comparisons between different *states of the same system,* as to how those different states affect the well-being of *the same set of individuals.* It is not designed to compare *different systems* which contain *different individuals.*

Nonetheless, one might attempt to extend the Pareto Superiority Principle to intersystemic efficiency comparisons by developing the concept of a *representative* (or typical) state of a given system. The idea would be to pick out a representative state of one system and a representative state of another system and then to compare the systems by determining whether the representative state of one was Pareto Superior to the representative state of the other. But developing the notion of a representative state adequate for such comparisons may be difficult.

Even if the concept of a representative state of a system can be adequately developed, however, there is a much more serious problem. Suppose that we are attempting to compare the Soviet system with the American system by applying the Pareto Superiority Principle to their respective representative states. Presumably we are to ask whether at least one individual in the representative state of one system is better off than anyone in the representative state of the other system while none in the representative state of the first system is worse off than anyone in the representative state of the second system. Since the different systems contain different groups of people, answering this question requires us to make interpersonal utility comparisons— to compare one individual's well-being with that of another. But one of the main reasons for adopting the Pareto Superiority Principle in the first place, it must be recalled, was that its use avoids interpersonal utility comparisons. To that extent, this first approach to intersystemic efficiency comparisons seems unacceptable.

A second strategy attempts to reduce the problem of comparing two different types of systems to that of comparing two different states of the *same* system that has undergone a change from being a system of one type to being a system of another type. Suppose we wish to use the Pareto Superiority Principle to compare systems of type *A* (for example, market systems) with systems of type *B* (nonmarket socialist systems). We focus on a particular instance of a type *A* system; call it system 1. We then perform a thought experiment in which we imagine system 1 undergoing a transformation from being a type *A* system (in representative state R^a) to being a type *B* system (in representative state R^b)—for example, a transition from capitalism to nonmarket socialism. We then compare R^a (the representative state of 1 when 1 was a type *A* system) with R^b (the representative state of 1 when 1 has become a type *B* system). This way of making intersystemic efficiency comparisons attempts to avoid interpersonal utility comparisons by focusing on only one set of individuals (and asking whether at least one of those individuals would be better off in the one type of system than *he* would be in the other type, while no one would be worse off in the first system).

This second approach, however, is also vulnerable to a grave objection. It rests upon two dubious assumptions. The first is that the transformation from one type of social system to another does not radically alter the *interests* of the individuals in question. The second assumption is that we can determine in some reliable way whether or not an individual is better off in one state than in another even though his interests in the two states are *radically different.*

The first assumption would be unproblematic if what is in an individual's interest, that is, what contributes to his well-being, were given and fixed, independently of the type of social organization in which he lives. "Interests" may be construed either subjectively or objectively. According to the *purely subjective* notion of interests, something is in a person's interest only if he is interested in it. The purely subjective notion of interests identifies interests with preferences. Clearly, if interests are understood in this purely subjective way, then the sort of society in which one lives plays a very important role in determining what is in one's interest, because at least some of one's preferences as a member of one society will diverge sharply from some of one's preferences as a member of a quite different society.

At the other extreme, "interests" may be construed in a *purely objective* way. On this view what is in one's interest (that which if attained or realized will contribute to one's well-being) may be wholly divorced from what one prefers (that in which one takes an interest).

At least when applied to normal individuals of adequately developed powers of choice and deliberation, this purely objective view of interests has little to commend it. For although it is no doubt true that an individual may sometimes, because of ignorance or weakness of the will, fail to prefer or take an interest in something that is conducive to his well-being, it is not plausible to maintain that such an individual's well-being is in no way based, even in part, upon his actual preferences.

Nonetheless, even if an individual's interests are partly subjective, that is, not purely objective, they may still be partly objective in the following sense. There may be some things, such as an adequate minimum of food, shelter, and rest, in which virtually all people do in fact take an interest and there may be some states of affairs, such as the existence of some form of social cooperation, which are almost universally necessary for attaining these things. The interests in these goods and in the conditions for attaining them may properly be called objective interests. However, in any circumstances beyond those of mere subsistence, most individuals will regard these "objective goods" (such as food, shelter, and rest) not as ultimate ends, but as instrumentally valuable for the attainment of other things they prefer. And which ultimate ends an individual pursues—as well as how he relates them one to another in order of priority—may be greatly influenced by the social environment in which his scheme of goals is formulated. Hence even if what is conducive to an individual's well-being is in part determined by objective interests, it is a mistake to assume that the transformation from one type of social system to another does not radically alter the interests of the individuals in question.

The second assumption, that we can reliably determine whether or not an individual is better off in one society than another even though his interests in the two societies are radically different, may be challenged in either of two ways. The first, more extreme of these is to argue that if the change in an individual's interests wrought by a transformation of the social system is profound enough, then the conditions for the individual's personal identity are undercut. The assumption here is that it is the character of one's most fundamental interests that makes one the particular person one is. If the individual whom we called Jones in the type *A* system is a different person from the individual we call Jones in the type *B* system, then our thought experiment is of no avail. In comparing "Jones's" well-being before and after the transformation we will be comparing the well-being of two different persons. But recall, the purpose of the thought experiment was to develop a way of making intersystemic efficiency comparisons that did *not* involve interpersonal utility comparisons.

The line of argument, however, is open to a serious objection. According to a plausible theory of personal identity developed by John Perry, a person can survive even rather drastic changes in his interests.[16] This theory distinguishes between values, preferences, interests, and other features of what we commonly call personality, on the one hand, and the underlying properties or processes whose existence is postulated to account for the rather dramatic changes in the constituents of personality which may occur in the normal course of maturation and development over the individual's lifetime. The theory holds that so long as there is continuity in the *"substratum"* properties or processes, the same person persists, even if there are radical discontinuities in the "surface" psychological features. So if this view is correct, the same person might continue to exist even if a transformation of the social system produced a profound change in his interests.

The second way of challenging the assumption that we can reliably determine whether an individual is better off in one society than another even though his interests are radically different in the two societies does not depend on the claim that the conditions for personal identity have been undercut. The idea, rather, is that we cannot reliably judge that Jones is better off in society *A* than in society *B* unless there is a substantial common core of interests which Jones has in both societies.

It might be thought that the objective interests discussed earlier, the interest in food, shelter, and rest, suffice to serve as this common core. It is true that we may be confident in judging that Jones would be better off in society *A* if these basic interests were satisfied in *A* but not satisfied in *B*. However, once we are faced with the task of comparing Jones's well-being in two societies that both satisfy these basic interests, our confidence wanes if the differences in the other interests Jones has in the two societies are profound. Yet for the comparisons in which we are most interested—for example, comparisons between market systems and socialist or communist systems—both will presumably provide for basic interests.

We could confidently make the comparative judgments in question if in doing so we were simply objectively measuring different quantities of the same "stuff" in the two societies—magnitudes of pleasure, for example, where pleasure is thought of as a psychological state or a property of a psychological state. We have already seen, however, (in chapter 1) that even if well-being could be reduced to pleasure, there is no reason to restrict pleasure to a psychological state that could be quantitatively evaluated.

To avoid the problematic metaphysical assumption that in comparing Jones's well-being in two societies in which his interests are radically different we are objectively measuring different quantities of the same "stuff," we might instead attempt to rely upon Jones's *own* judgment as to his comparative well-being. One can certainly imagine an individual who lived through—and internalized—such a dramatic transformation of the social system himself rejecting any attempt to compare his state of well-being before and after the transformation. But even if he confidently claimed to be better off now than he was then, it is not obvious that we should consider his judgment well-grounded. For if he has truly internalized the values of the new social system and thereby not only abandoned but also repudiated the values of the old, he may no longer be capable of accurately appreciating the value of the life he used to live. If the discontinuity between his interests in society *A* and his interests in society *B* were profound, we might conclude that reliable comparisons of his states of well-being in the two societies were impossible, regardless of his confidence in his ability to make them.

We are most confident in comparing how well-off an individual is in one society with how well-off he is in another if there is a substantial core of interests common to both societies. In fact our confidence is greatest in those cases in which we assume that the interests relevant to the comparison are the same, since we typically limit our comparisons to some subset of the individual's interests. In other words, we more frequently make local and limited intrapersonal well-being comparisons rather than global, all-inclusive ones. We are usually more interested in knowing whether some change in an individual's situation has furthered or hindered certain of his interests rather than whether it has increased or decreased his well-being as such. These central cases of comparison are quite different from the problem of determining whether, say, the individual we now call Lee is happier living as a businessman in Hong Kong than he was living in the Stone Age culture into which he was born and in which he lived for twenty years on a remote island in the Philippines. Even if our criteria for personal identity allow us to say that *the same person* persisted through the change from one type of society to another, the change in the individual's interests may be so great that the problem is functionally equivalent to that of making *interpersonal* utility comparisons, strictly speaking.

Another, no less serious difficulty, is that even if the Pareto Superiority Principle could be extended to intersystemic comparisons without resurrecting the problem of interpersonal utility comparisons it was invoked to avoid, it is doubtful that the principle could provide a ranking of the types of systems we are most concerned to compare. Recall how stringent the Pareto Superiority Principle is: a state is Pareto Superior to another only if *no one* in the second state is worse off than he is in the first. Surely when a socialist claims that socialism is more efficient than capitalism he is not necessarily denying that some individuals (for example, the richest capitalists) will be disadvantaged by a transition to socialism. Nor do those who contend that capitalism is a more efficient system than socialism thereby commit themselves to defending the equally implausible thesis that transforming a socialist system into a capitalist system would worsen no one's condition, not even that of the most privileged party bureaucrat. Just as the Pareto Optimality Principle tends to be useless when applied to nontrivial policy decisions within a given society because in the difficult cases each option will affect someone adversely, so the Pareto Superiority Principle seems just as unhelpful if we attempt to use it to evaluate a transformation of the entire social order. To imagine that it would be otherwise is to be naively optimistic about the problem of harmonizing interests.

A third proposal for making intersystemic efficiency comparisons is designed to avoid the problem of changes in the individual's interests by abstracting entirely from the content of the individual's preferences. The suggestion is that we can compare different systems by comparing the *preference-satisfaction ratios* of the same individuals in the two systems.[17] The preference-satisfaction ratio, S/P for an individual, i, in a system, A, is the proportion of i's satisfied preferences to his total set of preferences. Thus we may compare two systems A and B as follows: if all (or most) individuals would have a higher preference-satisfaction ratio in A than in B, then A is the more efficient system. This way of making intersystemic efficiency comparisons, like the second formulation of the Pareto Optimality and Pareto Superiority principles just stated (in terms of preferences), assumes that the satisfaction of an individual's preferences either constitutes or at least accurately corresponds to his well-being. The virtue of this third approach is that we can compare preference-satisfaction ratios even if there are radical changes in the individual's interests.

There is, however, a very serious limitation on the usefulness of the notion of preference-satisfaction ratios in making intersystemic efficiency comparisons. Suppose, for example, that in society A, individual i has 100 preferences, and that in society A, 10 of those preferences are satisfied. Suppose that in society B, individual i would have only 5 preferences, but four of the 5 preferences would be satisfied in society B. The preference-satisfaction ratio for individual i in society A is 1:10 (that is .1), while in society B, i's preference-satisfaction ratio is 4:5 (that is, .8). But surely it does not follow that *i* is better off in society *B* than in society *A*. For one thing, the quality of satisfaction of the preferences that are satisfied in *A* might be higher than the quality of satisfaction of the preferences satisfied in *B*. It might be possible, for example, to reduce an individual's set of preferences to a very basic, easily satisfiable minimum, through psychosurgery, mind-altering drugs, or through brainwashing techniques. But even if a higher proportion of these limited preferences were satisfied, it would not follow that the individual would be better off. Comparisons of preference-satisfaction ratios in different systems can perhaps provide a rough indication of relative efficiency among systems, but the tenuousness of the connection between preference-satisfaction ratios and individual well-being restricts their usefulness considerably.

Yet a fourth approach would be to abandon the Pareto Superiorty Principle altogether, acknowledging that when used in intersystemic comparisons it fails to avoid the problem of interpersonal utility comparisons or provides no ranking of interestingly different systems. Instead, only the Pareto Optimality Principle would be employed. One might argue that one system is more efficient than another if the first *more frequently* attains Pareto Optimal outcomes than the second (or if its representative state is more frequently Pareto Optimal). The virtue of this approach is that it does avoid interpersonal utility comparisons.

The simple but fundamental problem with this approach is that it is unlikely that *any* real world systems, or at least any of the real world systems we are interested in comparing, *ever* reach a Pareto Optimal state. In every case, some if not all of the ideal conditions that guarantee Pareto Optimality are imperfectly satisfied, and this is true regardless of whether the system in question is a capitalistic (that is, private property) market system, a centralized socialist system (such as the USSR), or a mixed system with some centralized planning plus decentralized decision-making among competing firms (as in Yugoslavia). The Principle of Pareto Optimality is a binary evaluative criterion: a state is either Pareto Optimal or it is not. There is no such thing as being more or less Pareto Optimal. Efficiency in this sense does not admit of degrees nor, strictly speaking, of any comparison at all.

In general there is no uncontroversial, reliable, and even reasonably precise method for determining how much overall benefit is lost in a given system, at a particular time, due to failure to achieve Pareto Optimality, nor for determining the relative contributions to lost overall benefit which various sources of inefficiency make. Moreover, any attempt to determine how much loss of possible benefit can be attributed to a particular source of inefficiency, or to determine how much overall loss of possible benefit the system suffers as a result of various inefficiencies would require interpersonal utility comparisons, since both of these determinations would involve summing up benefits (utility) across different individuals.

It is important not to underestimate the significance of these points for arguments for or against the market on grounds of efficiency. It is not simply that there are practical difficulties (lack of information, for example) which hinder intersystemic efficiency comparisons. Rather, there is not even a *theory* of intersystemic efficiency comparisons in the same sense in which there is a theory of intrasystemic efficiency comparisons. All arguments concerning the relative efficiency of rival systems of social organization would appear to have an irreducibly intuitive element, though this is not to say that statements about the relative efficiency of various systems are arbitrary. At best we can identify various sources of inefficiency that occur in one system, see whether they, or other sources of inefficiency occur in the rival system, and then try to make some rather rough-and-ready estimate of how serious these inefficiencies are.

I have not attempted to prove the impossibility of coherent, well-supported comparisons of different types of economic systems on grounds of efficiency. My aim has been the much more modest one of showing, first, that efficiency arguments for or against the market depend ultimately upon such comparisons and, second, that there are very serious, and often unappreciated, obstacles to making them, especially in cases in which the systems to be compared differ dramatically.

There is an interesting argument which might to some extent mitigate this skeptical conclusion. We have a theory of the ideal market system that is powerful enough to allow us to prove that an ideal market system achieves Pareto Optimality. However, we do not have a theory of an ideal nonmarket system on the basis of which to prove that this ideal nonmarket system achieves Pareto Optimality. Therefore, even though no actual market system satisfies the conditions of the ideal market system, the *reasonable presumption* is that actual market systems are more efficient than actual nonmarket systems. Let us call this the some theory is better than no theory argument.[18]

David Friedman advances this argument and offers an analogy to illuminate it. Suppose you wish to fire a cannon at a distant target. You have had an elementary physics course which includes a theory of the trajectory of an ideal projectile—the path which a point mass will traverse in a vacuum in a uniform gravitational field. Of course the cannon ball is not a point mass (it has extension), and the path it follows will not be in a vacuum (it travels through the air, with friction), and the earth's gravitational field is not uniform. But nonetheless it surely would be more reasonable to aim the cannon at the angle arrived at by calculating according to the ideal theory than to choose an angle at random! Similarly, our best shot at efficiency is to choose a system which at least approximates the ideal of efficiency— a system for which there is a theory capable of generating an efficiency theorem—rather than one for which there is no such theory. Thus the burden of argument must lie on the advocate of a nonmarket system to show that such a system is more efficient. And in the absence of a developed theory of the nonmarket system, that burden of argument cannot be borne successfully. So we must conclude that a market system is more efficient.

The argument can be strengthened. One advantage of choosing a system for which there is a theory capable of generating an efficiency theorem is that that theory will provide us with guidance as to how we can modify the nonideal system so as to bring it closer to the ideal conditions that guarantee efficiency. The theory of the ideal market system explains which features of nonideal market systems (for example, monopoly) produce inefficiencies and hence tells us how to bring our nonideal market system closer to the ideal of efficiency. If no comparably powerful theory is available for the nonmarket system, then we know that it is highly probable that the system is inefficient, but we lack theoretical guidance for improving its efficiency. Again, some theory seems better than no theory, even if reality is only a distant approximation of the system described in the theory.

This argument might conclusively show that a nonideal market system is likely to be more efficient than a nonmarket alternative if (a) there was in fact no theory of nonmarket social organization, and if (b) there was no empirical evidence to show that nonmarket systems better approximate the ideal of efficiency than a random allocation would. However, neither of these assumptions seems to be justified. As we shall see in a critical discussion of the "Socialist Calculation Debate" in Chapter 4, there is a theory of the planned socialist, nonmarket economy powerful enough to generate an efficiency theorem. It has been demonstrated mathematically by Pareto and E. Barone that such a system can duplicate the Pareto Optimal outcomes of the ideal market system. Further, the recent economic records of largely nonmarket systems such as the Soviet Union, though far from admirable, do not reveal economic chaos or even lack of growth, and from this it seems reasonable to conclude that these systems at least approximate efficiency more closely than a purely random allocation would.

So even if it would be more reasonable to choose a nonideal market system over a random "nonsystem," we cannot confidently conclude that any actual market system, no matter how imperfect, is preferable, on grounds of efficiency, to all nonmarket systems. Further, even if we could draw this conclusion, the argument would still not show that even greater efficiency cannot be achieved by selective intervention to minimize externalities and other market imperfections, or to re-distribute income the market process yields, by intervening in nonideal market systems. In other words, we would still be left with the problem of determining whether a more-regulated or a less-regulated, nonideal market would be more efficient.

The conclusion to be drawn is not that the notion of efficiency is useless, of course. But it does seem clear that we are on much firmer ground in asking whether a relatively minor, incremental change (which would not produce a new system but only a modification of an old one) would be more efficient, than we are when we facilely claim that one system is more efficient than a quite different system. However, this counsel of caution will seem to some to have unfortunately conservative implications: efficiency arguments for radical change, as opposed to reform, appear to be shaky if not impossible.

Many who advocate the use of the Paretian concept of efficiency for comparing systems do so because they believe attempts to compare systems on ethical grounds are afflicted by an irreducible relativism: it seems to them that all such ethical judgments are valid only within the assumptions of a particular system of ethical principles and that there are no rational grounds for choosing one such system over another. They have failed to notice that the problem of relativism is no less serious for comparative efficiency judgments than for com-parative ethical judgments.

3

Moral Arguments For and Against the Market

This chapter examines what may be broadly classified as moral arguments, as distinct from efficiency arguments, for and against the market. Disagreement about what it is for something to be a moral view may cast doubt upon the inclusion of certain arguments in favor of the market under this heading. For example, a defense of the market as a *mutually advantageous* arrangement might be regarded either as a *moral* argument, based on an ethical principle requiring that social arrangements are to be mutually advantageous, or as a *prudential* (that is, rationally self-interested) argument to the effect that the safest arrangement is one which is mutually advantageous. A moral argument from mutual advantage might be based ultimately upon a fundamental moral value of equal respect for persons, whereas a prudential argument might be grounded ultimately in self-interest, in the recognition that we are all vulnerable and that consequently one's safest strategy is to opt for an arrangement which guarantees that no one will be excluded from the benefits of social cooperation.

Even the earlier "nonmoral" arguments that focused on the inefficiencies of the market are often tacitly allied with moral arguments against it. Marx and more recent socialists who decry what they take to be the inefficiency or underproductivity of the market system are not making a purely technical assessment. Nor is their point simply that it is irrational to persist in an inefficient system when a more efficient one is practically possible. Such critics believe that it is not merely irrational but also immoral or at least inhumane to fail to replace a system whose inefficiency or underproductivity prevents important human needs from being met or important human potentials from being actualized.

Marx apparently also believed that there is another important connection between questions of efficiency and the moral evaluation of the market. His view seems to be that the basic civil and political legal rights which individuals enjoy in capitalism are valuable *only* as ways of coping with those sorts of conflicts of interest that are themselves artifacts of the capitalist system. Marx seems to have believed that basic civil and political rights, as well as distributive rights to a share of material wealth, are necessary and hence valuable only where there are class-divisions and the egoism to which class-divisions give rise, under conditions of scarcity. Since he also believed that communism will end class-divisions and greatly reduce egoism and scarcity, he believed that conceptions of rights will not play a significant role in communism, the form of social organization which he believed would replace capitalism.

This prediction of the obsolescence of conceptions of rights, and the implied rejection of the ultimate value of rights, rests upon a prediction that there is a nonmarket system of social organization which will be so efficient as to reduce greatly scarcity and the clashes of interest to which scarcity gives rise. In order to justify this prediction, the Marxist who rejects the market system and the moral framework of civil and political rights with which it is associated, must execute three ambitious tasks which so far remain uncompleted. First, he must develop a theory of nonmarket social organization in sufficient detail, and with sufficient explanatory power, to show how the problems of allocation, production, and distribution can be solved without the aid of the market as a coordinating device (and without the use of unacceptable levels of coercion, as in totalitarianism, state socialist systems). Second, he must show that such a system would be efficient enough to reduce significantly the problem of scarcity. Third, the Marxist must also show that the nonmarket system is not only coherent in theory but psychologically and politically feasible. Once again, we see that moral arguments and arguments from efficiency, though distinct, can be intimately related.

For our purposes, it will not be necessary to distinguish sharply between prudential and moral arguments or to try to answer perennial questions about the relationship between prudence (broadly construed as rational self-interest) and morality. Instead, it should suffice to use the rough label "moral arguments" to distinguish a rather diverse collection of arguments from those which are based on notions of efficiency.

The Social Darwinist Argument

In the late nineteenth century some defenders of the market attempted to utilize what they took to be the basic insights of Darwin's evolutionary biology. Social Darwinists viewed the market as an arena of conflict in which the "fittest" emerge as victors. According to this way of thinking, the market is the most "natural" form of social organization because it most closely resembles the natural world as it exists independently of human intervention.[1]

If this attempt to extend the evolutionary model of explanation to the economic sphere limited itself to explanation, it could not serve as a practical argument in favor of the market; and as a purely explanatory model it would stand or fall solely on the basis of its explanatory merit, but would have no implications for what we ought to do. For example, one might endeavor to explain the characteristics that long-standing, successful firms possess by showing that those characteristics are "selected" by competition. In other words, it might prove illuminating to show that possession of those characteristics enabled the firm in question to survive and flourish, or, to state the same point negatively, to show that a firm which did not possess these characteristics would have been destroyed by competition.

The extent to which the evolutionary explanatory model fits existing market systems is an empirical question. However, even if this model does provide the best explanation of a given market system, it does not follow that a system which fits the explanatory model is *preferable* to one which does not. As an argument for the market—as opposed to an explanation of it—the Social Darwinist view must provide *normative* as well as explanatory theses. It must be shown that the notion of evolution through competition *ought* to guide social policy and it must be shown that this notion actually provides substantive, practical guidance.

Proponents of the Social Darwinist argument usually claim that the redistributive arrangements of the welfare state ought to be dismantled, and that the market ought to be allowed to operate freely, because such interventions in the market interfere with the natural struggle for survival and hinder the operation of the law of the survival of the fittest. This position, however, is based on several misconceptions. First of all, the notion of fitness must always be understood as fitness *relative to* or *for* a particular environment or range of environments. For example, a person who is deficient in upper body strength may be as fit for clerical work as a weightlifter, and a myopic individual in a society which provides corrective lenses may be fully fit for almost any task. The programs of the welfare state can be viewed as strategies designed to enable individuals to survive and flourish, in part by modifying the individuals themselves (for example, through publicly subsidized education), and in part by modifying the environment (for example, through publicly subsidized sanitation services). Whether or not these strategies are successful is of course a controversial question, but the Social Darwinist cannot merely dismiss them as interferences with natural selection through competition. They are no more or less unnatural or artificial than the social and legal framework of the market itself.

Consequently, the conjunction of the statement that competition in the market selects the fittest and the statement that only the fittest survive yields no practical guidance. If it is to have any practical force at all, the Social Darwinist argument must show either that (1) the market system best promotes the survival of the species and that this criterion of survival alone is relevant for evaluating social systems, or that (2) the individuals who survive competition in the market possess certain characteristics that are desirable *independently* of their contribution to survival. Marshaling adequate empirical evidence for the first part of thesis (1) would be a very tall order indeed. It seems quite implausible to maintain that the human species can only survive in one particular type of social system. On the other hand, if the Social Darwinist's claim is that the market provides the *best* chances for survival, it still would not follow that the market is preferable overall, even if this claim were substantiated, simply because there are other worthy values besides maximization of survival prospects. And because there are, conduciveness to survival cannot provide a decisive criterion for choosing the market system over its rivals.

The thesis that (2) the traits selected by competition in the market are especially valuable may be understood in either of two ways. Either they are to be thought of as (a) traits whose existence is beneficial to all (or almost all) members of society, or they are to be thought of as (b) being intrinsically valuable or valuable solely to those who possess them. If the claim is that the existence of the traits in question is beneficial for all (even those who do not possess them), then it looks as if the normative basis of the Social Darwinist position has nothing to do with the notion of evolution or with that of survival as such. Instead the practical force of the view—that is, its significance for deciding whether to support, alter or abolish the market—rests upon the assumption of a principle of mutual advantage, a requirement that society ought to be arranged so as to be advantageous to all. The value of the market, then, is not that it avoids interference with the struggle for survival of the fittest, but rather that the selective process that occurs in the market system is the best means for fostering those traits whose existence benefits everyone (or at least the majority). On this interpretation, then, the Social Darwinist argument reduces to an argument from the Principle of Mutual Benefit; or, more accurately, evolutionary theory is used in a purely explanatory fashion to show how the assumed goal of mutual benefit can best be achieved.

On the second interpretation, (b) (that the traits selected by competition in the market are intrinsically valuable or valuable only to those who possess them), the Social Darwinist is committed to the thesis that the market is preferable to alternative systems because it does the best job of fostering certain traits which are preeminently valuable, independently of whether they contribute to the benefit of all. The characteristics usually cited are independence, industriousness, daring, imagination, self-discipline, and other character traits which defenders of the market associate with successful entrepreneurship.

There are at least two major difficulties with this version of the argument. First, critics of the market argue that so far as these traits are really desirable, or so far as they are expressed in morally acceptable ways, they are certainly not limited to individuals who live in a market system. Moreover, even if market competition does nurture characteristics that are desirable in themselves or for their possessors, it also encourages their misuse and fosters objectionable traits such as avarice, insensitivity to others, and duplicity. Indeed even some of the most famous defenders of the market, such as Bernard Mandeville and Adam Smith, have admitted that it does breed unsavory and even morally objectionable traits; but they have concluded that this corruption of character is worth the price of increased productivity and the greater potential mutual benefit which this allows.

The second difficulty arises if one makes the assumption that the traits which the market fosters are not in fact beneficial for all. For it is difficult to see why a loser in the competitive struggle should support the market system when it encourages the development of character traits whose existence in others works to his disadvantage and which he himself does not possess to any significant degree.

The Argument from Desert

It is sometimes argued that the market system is preferable because it distributes wealth according to desert.[2] This claim is ambiguous. On the one hand, it may mean that the market distributes wealth in proportion to the individual's exhibition of meritorious behavior (for example, hard work and self-sacrifice) or possession of meritorious character traits (such as effort and frugality). On the other hand, it may mean that the market distributes wealth according to the individual's contribution to society or to the good of others. The second interpretation singles out contribution to others as the appropriate criterion for desert, while the first recognizes that there may be several different types of desert. But both assume that the market *does* distribute wealth according to desert and both assume that wealth *should* be distributed according to desert.

The first interpretation may easily be challenged on purely factual grounds. It is undeniable that luck often plays an important role in determining whether or not one acquires and keeps wealth in the market. People sometimes reap "windfall profits" by sheer guesswork or even by making investment choices which, granted the available information at the time, were wildly irrational. More importantly, a person's share of wealth is often heavily influenced by the financial and social position of his parents and to that extent is undeserved. Further, as was observed earlier in examining the Social Darwinist argument, the proportion of wealth a person obtains in the market system sometimes depends upon his possession of undesirable traits such as avarice and duplicity—characteristics which we do not think of as appropriate bases for desert.

The second interpretation of the argument from desert, which identifies desert with contribution to the good of others, is also weak. It rests on two assumptions: (1) that the share of wealth a person obtains in the market system is proportional to his marginal productivity (the additional amount of "output" he produces, granted each additional amount of "input" above some specified initial level of "inputs"), and (2) that a person's marginal productivity is a sufficiently accurate measure of his contribution to the good of others to serve as an acceptable basis for determining the share of wealth he deserves.

The first assumption overlooks an important fact about human beings, whether they live in a market system or not. All human beings, for a significant part of their lives, are dependent on others for the satisfaction of their needs, even though they are at that time incapable of being producers who contribute to satisfying the needs of others. To state that the market distributes wealth according to marginal productivity (or according to any other alleged basis of desert) is simply to overlook the fact that human beings do not spring full-blown into the world as independent exchangers in the market. Instead, they begin life as children and the share of wealth they receive in this period of largely unproductive dependency cannot by any stretch of the imagination be correlated with their marginal productivity or with their contribution to the good of others.

The second assumption, that marginal productivity is a sufficiently accurate measure of contribution to others to serve as a basis for distribution according to desert, is also dubious. Unless one is willing to embrace an implausible, radically subjectivist concept of well-being, the mere fact that someone is productive in the sense of enabling others to satisfy their preferences does not show that what he gets from them in return is proportional to his contribution to their well-being. Those who produce and sell cigarettes or heroin or other clearly dangerous products may exhibit high-marginal productivity and their income may in fact reflect this marginal productivity. But it does not follow that the income they receive is proportional to what they contribute to the well-being of others. And once the problem of externalities (whether positive or negative) is acknowledged, it is even less plausible to assume that an individual's marginal productivity, which does not reflect externalities, is an accurate measure of his contribution to the good of others.

Both interpretations of the argument from desert are liable to a much more fundamental objection. Why should we assume in the first place that one's overall share of wealth should be determined by desert in any sense? Some of the more sophisticated advocates of the market have in fact thought it to be a consideration in favor of the market that it does *not* distribute wealth according to merit. Their point is that a society in which wealth is thought to be distributed in accordance with desert would be oppressive and excessively demanding. In such a system, the worse off, in addition to suffering from the material disadvantages of having less wealth than others, would bear the social stigma (and perhaps the diminished sense of self-worth) of being seen as morally inferior as well.

Finally, the assumption that wealth ought to be distributed according to desert can also be challenged once we distinguish between what a person *deserves* and what he is *entitled to*. According to some moral theories of property rights, an individual may be entitled to something or have a right to it, even though he cannot be said to deserve it. The force of this objection to the argument from desert depends ultimately upon the plausibility of the theory of rights or entitlements on the basis of which it is advanced. Later we will examine a libertarian or Lockean theory of moral rights which rejects the assumption that wealth should be distributed according to desert but which supports the market on the grounds that people are entitled to whatever they get through voluntary exchanges, so long as their initial holdings were justly acquired.

Arguments from Mutual Advantage and
Utilitarian Arguments

It was noted earlier that one version of the argument for the market from desert identifies desert with contribution to the good of others. A more plausible view is that although the ultimate justification of the market is that (1) the system *as a whole* maximizes overall utility, or (2) the system as a whole contributes to the good of all, there is no close correlation between the share of wealth an individual receives in the market and *that individual's* contribution to the good of others. In other words, one can argue for the market either on utilitarian grounds or on grounds of mutual benefit, without assuming that the market distributes wealth according to individual contribution or according to individual marginal productivity, and without assuming that an individual's marginal productivity is an accurate measure of his contribution to the well-being of others.

Some defenders of the market tend to blur the distinction between the utilitarian argument (1) and the argument from mutual advantage (2). However, it is important to emphasize that what maximizes social utility may not be *mutually* advantageous. It is at least possible, as critics of utilitarianism often point out, that a system which provided great benefits for some at the expense of deprivation and slavery for others would maximize overall utility. All that is necessary is that the benefits to the privileged class exceed the costs to the exploited and that there be no alternative arrangement that would yield greater net utility overall. To put the matter in a slightly different way: mutual benefit and overall utility maximization are conceptually distinct and may diverge in practice because mutual advantage requires that some benefits be distributed to all, while overall utility maximization places no constraints on how benefits are distributed so long as the total net amount of benefits is as high as possible. For this reason the two arguments for the market will be considered separately, beginning with the utilitarian argument.

Utilitarianism: For and Against the Market   Utilitarianism, as a comprehensive moral theory which purports to govern individual conduct as well as social institutions, may be of either of two types: Act Utilitarianism or Rule Utilitarianism. Act Utilitarianism defines rightness by reference to particular acts. An act is right if and only if it maximizes net overall (that is, social) utility. Rule Utilitarianism defines rightness by reference to rules of action and makes the rightness of particular acts depend upon the rules under which those acts fall. A rule is right if and only if general compliance with that rule (or with a set of rules of which it is an element) maximizes net social utility, and a particular action is right if and only if it falls under such a rule. Both Act and Rule Utilitarianism may be versions of either Classical or Average Utilitarianism. Classical Utilitarianism defines the rightness of acts or rules as maximization of *aggregate utility*; Average Utilitarianism defines rightness as maximization of *utility per capita*. The aggregate utility produced by an act or by general compliance with a rule is the sum of the utility produced for each individual affected, minus the sum of the disutility produced for each individual affected. Average utility is net aggregate utility divided by the number of individuals affected. *Utility* is defined as pleasure, satisfaction, happiness, or the satisfaction of preferences, as the latter are revealed through individuals' choices. Since Classical Utilitarianism has historically been the dominant form of the theory and since the market can be thought of as a complex institution structured by rules, including laws and less formal social norms, I shall concentrate on the Classical Rule Utilitarian argument for the market. But for economy the qualifier 'Classical Rule' will generally be omitted in what follows. According to the utilitarian argument, the justification of the market is that general compliance with the rules that constitute the social and legal framework of the market maximizes social utility.[3]

Some of the most prominent advocates of the market have defended it on utilitarian grounds; others have used utilitarianism to attack the market. This is not surprising, granted the complexity of the empirical data necessary for determining whether the market system does in fact maximize utility.

Utilitarians who criticize the market and advocate either abandoning it in favor of socialism or intervening in the market by modifying and supplementing it with government welfare programs usually do so on one or both of two grounds: (1) they argue that actual markets fail to approximate sufficiently the efficiency of the ideal market (in particular because of externalities and public goods problems); or (2) they contend that the *unequal* distribution produced by the market fails to maximize social utility, even when outcomes are Pareto Optimal, because redistributing some wealth and income from the better off to the worse off would increase the utility of the worse off more than it would decrease the utility of the better off. We have already seen, in chapter 1, that it is not possible to make well-supported, sweeping generalizations about whether or not government intervention in the market will or will not reduce externalities or solve public goods problems in an efficient way. Utilitarians are often divided in their assessment of whether the costs of government intervention would outweigh the benefits in a particular case.

The argument that maximizing social utility requires a more equal distribution than the market can be expected to produce rests upon a disputable assumption: that all individuals can be viewed, for purposes of calculating social utility, as having the same capacity for enjoyment. To be more precise, egalitarian, antimarket utilitarians assume that wealth and income (or the goods and services they can buy) have diminishing marginal utility for everyone and that social utility will be maximized if, for purposes of determining social policy, we proceed as if the threshold at which marginal utility begins to decline and that the rate of its decline are the same for all. The idea is that although there are differences in the marginal utility curves of individuals, we lack accurate knowledge of them, and at any rate they tend to cancel each other out when large numbers of individuals are considered. Given the assumption of equal diminishing marginal utility, utilitarianism seems to require a more equal distribution than the unfettered market would yield.

There is a second, stronger utilitarian argument for distributing income equally. Even if we acknowledge that there may be significant differences among individuals' diminishing marginal utilities for income, we have no reliable way of determining, for any pair of individuals, who has the greater diminishing marginal utility for income at any given distribution of income we might specify. Suppose we distribute available income equally. Granted our state of ignorance about the differences in individuals' marginal utilities for income, the probability that a shift in one direction away from equality would increase overall utility is equal to the probability that a shift in the opposite direction would increase overall utility, at least if very large numbers of shifts away from equality are involved. For example, suppose we divide $200 between individual A and individual B. Suppose that we then shift the distribution so that A now has $120 and B has $80. In the absence of knowledge about their diminishing marginal utilities for income, the probability that such a shift away from equality will increase overall utility is equal to the probability that it would decrease overall utility, at least if we are considering a very large number of possible shifts. However, even if the probability of a loss of utility is equal to the probability of a gain of utility, the probable *magnitude* of the loss of utility is greater than the probable *magnitude* of the gain. The reason for this becomes clear from Figure 3.1.[4]

Curves AA' and BB' represent the *marginal* utilities of income for individuals A and B respectively. Notice that the curves are both downward sloping, indicating that income has diminishing marginal

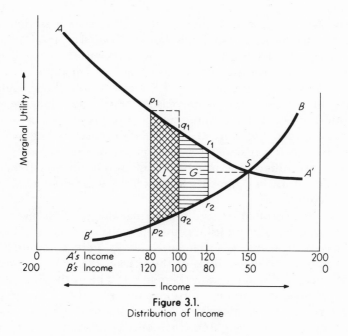

Figure 3.1.
Distribution of Income

utility for both. Individual A's marginal utility curve is higher than B's, indicating that he has a greater capacity for reaping satisfaction from a given amount of income than B. The vertical line passing through q_1 and q_2 represents an equal distribution of the total income $200 ($100 for A, $100 for B). At that distribution, A's marginal utility, q_1, is greater than B's marginal utility, q_2.

By hypothesis we know that A and B have different utilities for income but we do not know whose utility is greater. Suppose that in this state of ignorance we can choose either of two unequal distributions (two departures from the distribution which gives A and B $100.00 each): either we give A $120.00 and B $80.00, or we give B $120.00 and A $80.00. (Of course if we knew that A has higher utility for income than B, we would choose the former unequal distribution, but by hypothesis we don't know this.)

The horizontally shaded area, G, represents the *gain* in overall utility achieved by departing from the equal distribution and giving A $120 and B $80. The double-shaded area, L, represents the *loss* of overall utility incurred by departing from equality to give B $120 and A $80. Because the individuals' marginal utility curves slope downward—that is, because diminishing marginal utility for income is assumed—the potential losses from departures from an equal distribution are greater than the potential gains (the area L is larger than the area G). Therefore, if we know that income has diminishing marginal utility, but do not know how individuals' marginal utilities for income differ from one another, we maximize expected (that is, probable) overall utility by distributing income equally.

Utilitarians who argue in favor of the market reject the egalitarian line for one or more of three reasons. First, they may reject the assumption of equal diminishing marginal utility, either because, like Plato, they believe that there are natural differences among individuals which affect their capacities for enjoyment, or because they believe that there are differences which, though rooted in social conditions rather than natural endowments, are not likely to be eliminated without excessive costs.

Second, the promarket utilitarian may argue that even if the assumption of equal diminishing marginal utility is accurate enough for purposes of assessing social institutions, there is another factor which supports the inequalities of the market, namely, the *production effects* of unequal distribution in the market. This is the familiar claim that the prospect of gaining more income or wealth through greater expenditure of effort and greater risk-taking provides the individual with an incentive for heightened productivity, which in turn results in increased social utility. If diminishing marginal utility is assumed to be equal and if the size of the economic pie is assumed to be fixed, then an equal distribution would maximize social utility. But if the size of the pie and hence the utility obtainable from it can be expanded though the incentives to productivity provided by an unequal distribution, then an unequal distribution maximizes social utility. This inegalitarian, promarket, utilitarian argument itself rests on two controversial empirical assumptions: (1) that a feasible egalitarian (non-market) system could not provide effective incentives for productivity, and (2) that the degree of inequality that results from the market does not exceed the degree of inequality required for effective incentives for productivity.

Third, utilitarians who favor the market may also argue that even if a more egalitarian system could solve the problem of production incentives, the concentration of government power it would require would itself have effects that are detrimental to the individual's liberty to pursue effectively his own happiness, with the result that social utility would not be maximized.

The contention that the market is preferable to alternative systems because it minimizes the concentration of power in general and the growth of government power in particular is not unique to utilitarian defenses of the market. It is also advanced by moral rights theorists who value civil and political liberties independently of whether protecting them maximizes social utility. The claim that the market provides the best safeguard for civil and political liberties will be examined in detail later in this chapter. But this much can be said about the utilitarian version of this argument for the market: as in the case of externalities and public goods problems, a "shotgun" approach seems highly implausible. It is much more probable that a utilitarian analysis that is well-grounded in reliable empirical data will conclude that in some areas a relatively unfettered market will be best, while in others either government provision of goods and services or, more likely, government intervention in the market, will maximize utility. In particular, whether a given increase in government power will seriously undermine individual liberties must surely depend upon the character of the existing power structure and the prevailing economic conditions, as well as the social, cultural, and political traditions of the group in question.

Some utilitarians, impressed with the cogency of utilitarian arguments for and against the market, and chary of sweeping generalizations on one side or the other, have concluded that maximizing social utility requires a relatively large role for the market plus a minimal welfare program or "safety net" or "decent minimum" of basic goods and services guaranteed for all who cannot attain them for themselves. The attractions of this approach are considerable. On the one hand, reserving a large role for the market acknowledges the efficiency of that system, including heightened productivity resulting from unequal distribution and the minimization of government power. On the other hand, supplementing the distributive shares of the worse off by a safety net or decent minimum system acknowledges that, at least for minimal amounts of certain basic goods such as food and shelter, marginal utility is relatively uniform for all individuals. The trick, of course, is to set the level of taxation needed to provide the safety net high enough to reap utilities that would not be obtainable in the more inegalitarian distribution of an unfettered market but low enough to avoid excessive reductions of incentives for productivity.

Even if maximizing social utility would require a government-backed, decent minimum program, it does not follow that maximizing utility would justify a guaranteed decent minimum for *everyone*.[5] To appreciate this important point an example may be helpful.

Those who advocate a guaranteed decent minimum (on utilitarian or other grounds) usually contend that the decent minimum will include subsistence levels of goods such as food and shelter along with at least the more basic medical services. It is not clear, however, that maximizing social utility would require that these goods and services be guaranteed to everyone, including those who suffer severe disabilities. The class of newborns with Down's Syndrome (formerly called Mongolism), for example, might well be excluded from the guaranteed decent minimum on utilitarian grounds. These retarded individuals, who often suffer from serious physical disabilities as well, tend to require a large outlay of social resources over the course of their lives. Relative to the costs of caring for them, the contribution these individuals make to social utility is not large, at least so far as we are limited to a conception of contribution that makes it quantifiable. If this is the case, then, utilitarianism will justify—indeed will require—that these individuals be excluded from the guaranteed decent minimum.[6]

Two points must be emphasized. The first is that these infants are capable of enjoyment. Unlike more severely disabled individuals (such as those who become permanently comatose due to trauma, or anencephalics—babies born with no brain above the brain stem) Down's babies can achieve simple satisfactions. Nonetheless, because they tend to be economically less productive than mentally normal individuals, utilitarian calculations may lead to the conclusion that resources that would be used to provide them with a decent minimum could be better spent on others who will be more productive. The second point to be emphasized is that utilitarian calculations may lead us to exclude these disabled individuals from even the most basic care, not just expensive, high-technology care. In sum, utilitarianism may mandate that, even for the most basic goods and services, what is guaranteed for most individuals should not be provided for some, even though their needs are equal and they would benefit greatly from them.

It might be objected that such an exclusionary policy would not in fact maximize social utility because, granted fallibility in its administration and a public awareness of this fallibility, a great deal of disutility would result in the form of anxiety over the prospect of "false positives" in the selection of those who are to be excluded from the decent minimum. This reply is weak because membership in the excluded class can be reliably ascertained from birth (by a test for chromosomal anomaly) and because anyone who is intelligent enough to dread being misclassified has virtually nothing to fear. Further, if the policy were applied only to *newborn* Down's individuals, disutility to family members would be minimized because attachments would not yet be developed. Even though it is true that some Down's individuals, if allowed to survive, may make significant contributions to social utility, a selective exclusionary policy may be impractical, due to the difficulty of predicting at birth the degree of mental impairment. Finally, if a uniform exclusionary policy for Down's newborns were supported by a public education program to make clear the reliable utilitarian calculations that led to the exclusion of this special class, there would be no reason to assume that such a policy would inevitably lead us down a "slippery slope" to wholesale euthanasia.

It seems, then, that even if utilitarian arguments show that the market should be constrained and supplemented by a guaranteed decent minimum policy, it does not follow that *everyone* should be guaranteed a decent minimum. Once this qualification is acknowledged, however, there is a strong utilitarian case against the unfettered market and in favor of a large role for the market constrained and supplemented by a guaranteed decent minimum welfare program.

There are, however, two fundamental objections to the whole utilitarian approach—criticisms which purport to undermine utilitarian arguments for *or* against the market. The first, which we have already encountered, is the charge that the interpersonal utility comparisons which utilitarianism requires either cannot be made at all or cannot be made with sufficient accuracy to guide social policy. The popularity of the Paretian concept of efficiency, as we saw earlier, is in part an indication of how seriously this objection is taken, at least by most economists.

The utilitarian who acknowledges the problem of interpersonal utility comparisons can, however, advocate the use of the Pareto Superiority Principle on utilitarian grounds. For even though a move from a Pareto Inferior to a Pareto Superior state does not guarantee that net social utility is *maximized*, it does guarantee that there is at least an *increase* in net social utility.

Suppose we are comparing three states, S^1, S^2, and S^3. S^2 may be Pareto Superior to S^1 and S^3 may be Pareto Superior to S^1; yet it may still be the case that S^2 is not Pareto Superior to S^3 and that S^3 is not Pareto Superior to S^2. If this is so, and if S^2 and S^3 are the only feasible alternatives to S^1, then we know that moving to either S^2 or S^3 will *increase* net social utility relative to S^1, but we have no way of determining which move would *maximize* social utility. So, while the Pareto Superiority Principle cannot uniquely select the utility-maximizing policy (where there is more than one Pareto Superior alternative), it can tell us whether we are at least moving in the direction of maximizing utility. And this, the utilitarian can claim, is enough to make utilitarian social policy decisions possible.[7]

If our earlier argument concerning the barriers to intersystemic efficiency comparisons is cogent, however, the utilitarian should be reluctant to attempt to apply the Pareto Superiority Criterion across systems that differ in fundamental ways, since this merely in effect resurrects the problem of interpersonal utility comparisons he seeks to avoid. Yet even if recourse to the Pareto Superiority Principle succeeds against the charge that utilitarianism fails because it requires unobtainable utility comparisons, there is another basic objection to utilitarianism, and hence to utilitarian arguments for or against the market. This second type of objection, which is developed by John Rawls in his book, *A Theory of Justice*, is of a *moral*, rather than a technical nature.[8] Rawls argues that utilitarianism does not provide a secure foundation for basic civil and political liberties and that this deficiency rests, ultimately, upon utilitarianism's failure to take seriously the *separateness of persons*. According to utilitarianism, the ultimate objects of moral concern in the universe are desires or preferences, not persons or even individual sentient organisms. Rawls contends that the failure to recognize that persons are distinct both from one another and from their own desires inevitably leads to utilitarianism's inability to provide an adequate support for enforcing basic, individual civil and political rights. Just as utilitarian calculations may result in a policy of excluding certain individuals from a decent minimum of food, shelter, or basic medical services, so they may also prove inadequate for justifying a system of equal basic civil and political liberties for everyone. If utilitarianism is itself defective either on the technical ground that it requires unobtainable interpersonal utility comparisons or on the moral ground that it overlooks the separateness and significance of persons and hence cannot provide a firm foundation for basic individual rights—then utilitarian arguments for *or* against the market are to that extent undercut.

What, then, are we to conclude? The upshot is simply this: moral and technical objections to utilitarianism at the very least make it implausible to rely *exclusively* upon arguments about what will maximize social utility in attempts to evaluate the market system, and even if these technical and moral objections can be met, the empirical data required for a utilitarian evaluation of the market are so complex that a sweeping utilitarian judgment either in favor of or against the market seems unlikely. Nonetheless, utilitarian arguments may play a significant, though limited, role in attempts to make less global judgments about the proper scope and limits of the operation of the market.

Arguments from Mutual Advantage Some of those who find utilitarianism morally defective because it allows some individuals to be sacrificed so long as doing so benefits others sufficiently to maximize social utility, may for that reason reject utilitarian arguments in favor of the market and attempt instead to argue for the market on the grounds that it is a *mutually* advantageous system. Indeed, some of the most famous advocates of the market, such as John Locke and Adam Smith, may be resting their case upon a principle of mutual advantage rather than upon the Principle of Utility.

The claim that the market system is mutually advantageous, however, is ambiguous because advantage is a comparative notion. Depending upon what point of reference is specified for comparison, we get different interpretations of the Principle of Mutual Advantage. If the reference point is a hypothetical "state of nature" in which there is virtually no social cooperation, then it may be quite true that a market system, which allows exchanges and encourages division of labor and increased productivity, is mutually advantageous relative to that bleak and solitary condition. But this comparative claim is, of course, not sufficient to single out the market as uniquely preferable, since there may be many forms of social organization which make everyone better off than he would be if social cooperation were utterly absent. Standard criticisms of Hobbes's defense of the authoritarian state stress precisely this point. Hobbes argued that we are all better off in an authoritarian state than in a state of nature in which there is no stable framework of social cooperation.[9] One could agree with Hobbes that everyone is better off in an authoritarian state than with no state at all and yet deny that being mutually advantageous in this very minimal sense is sufficient to justify this particular system of social cooperation. Similarly, the fact that a more or less unfettered market system makes everyone better off than he would be if there were no system of social cooperation at all can hardly be enough by itself to legitimize the market.

If we conclude from this that we ought to strengthen the requirement of mutual advantage, what is the appropriate reference point? There seem to be two alternatives worth considering. On the one hand, a proponent of the market might argue that the market satisfies the criterion of being more advantageous than any feasible alternative system, including socialism of one sort or the other. Regardless of whether this use of the extremely strong reading of the Principle of Mutual Advantage is based ultimately upon prudential considerations (individual self-interest) or a moral value (equal concern or respect), it is very problematic because it requires us to make efficiency comparisons among fundamentally different systems. And these, we have already seen, are often dubious if not impossible to make. So any attempt to argue for the market on the basis of this first, extremely strong interpretation of the Principle of Mutual Advantage must overcome all of the difficulties we encountered earlier when we examined attempts to apply the Paretian notion of efficiency across significantly different systems.

On the other hand, the Principle of Mutual Advantage might be given the weaker interpretation considered earlier, and figure as only one factor in a more complex argument for the market. One might view the requirement that everyone be better off than in the non-cooperative situation as a *necessary* condition for choosing a system and then argue that among those systems that satisfy this necessary condition, the market system scores highest according to other important moral criteria. This more subtle use of the notion of mutual advantage seems closer to the defense of the market system actually offered by moral rights theorists such as Locke. Locke apparently held that the chief rationale for any form of social cooperation, including those which rely upon government as a coercive apparatus for resolving conflicts, is that they make us all better off than we would be were there no social cooperation. However, he also seems to have believed that mutual advantage in this weak sense is not enough to justify a social system. A mutually advantageous system of social cooperation must also respect and enforce certain basic moral rights if it is to warrant our allegiance.[10] Further, Locke is generally thought to have believed that only a relatively unfettered market system can do this.

The Argument from Lockean or Libertarian Moral Rights

Perhaps the most influential contemporary moral case for the market is that presented by Robert Nozick in his book *Anarchy, State, and Utopia*.[11] Although Nozick claims that the theory of rights he endorses is Lockean, there is a sense in which his defense of the market is much more radical than Locke's. Nozick does not seem to include the weak interpretation of the Principle of Mutual Advantage even as a necessary condition for the legitimacy of a social system. Instead, according to Nozick, what is decisive is that the market, and the market alone, avoids violations of what he takes to be basic moral rights. Nozick seems to think that the market is in fact a mutually advantageous system, at least relative to noncooperation, and that perhaps it is also more advantageous than any feasible alternative. But there is a sense in which all of this is merely icing on the cake. Even if the market system were not mutually advantageous, Nozick believes it would still be overwhelmingly preferable to any mutually advantageous system that violates individual rights. In other words, for Nozick, the requirement that individual rights must not be violated is the most basic consideration for choosing among systems, and this criterion by itself is sufficient to make the case for the market as being uniquely preferable.

There are a number of different libertarian theories, but their defining doctrine is that coercion (understood narrowly as physical force or the threat of physical force) may be used only to prevent or punish physical harm, theft, and fraud, and to enforce voluntary contracts. In Nozick's theory, as in libertarian theories generally, a very broad right to private property, including private property in the means of production, is morally fundamental and determines both the most basic principles of individual conduct and the legitimate role of the state. Since he believes that human beings will develop an extensive market system wherever the individuals' right to private property is respected and the state's role is limited to that of enforcing contracts and protecting against physical force, theft, and fraud, Nozick concludes that his moral theory provides the best defense of the market. Any attempt to interfere with the market by using the coercive power of the state to reduce inequality or even to provide a decent minimum by taxing some to benefit others violates the basic moral right to private property.

It is important to note that for Nozick, as for most other libertarian rights theorists, property rights are not restricted to ownership of external things. According to Nozick, individuals have a property right in their persons and in whatever "holdings" they acquire through actions that satisfy (1) the principle of justice in "initial acquisition," and (2) the principle of justice "in transfer." (1) specifies how a person can come to have a property right to previously unowned things without violating anyone else's property rights. Nozick's account of just initial acquisition draws heavily on Locke's view that a person comes to have a property right to natural objects by "mixing his labor" with them, that is, by improving them by his efforts.

While he does not succeed in formulating a principle of justice in initial acquisition, Nozick argues that it would have to include a proviso which places a limit on the holdings one can acquire. He says that one may exclusively appropriate as much of an unowned item as one desires so long as (a) one does not thereby worsen the conditions of others by creating a situation in which others are no longer able to use freely, without exclusively appropriating, what they previously could; or (b) one properly compensates everyone whose condition is worsened in the way specified in (a).[12] Nozick's proviso (which he derives from Locke) focuses only on one way in which a person's exclusive appropriation can worsen the condition of others. It does not prohibit exclusive appropriation or mandate compensation if one's appropriation worsens another's condition merely by limiting his opportunities to appropriate exclusively (rather than merely use in common) the thing in question.

The principle of justice in transfer (2) states that a person may transfer his justly acquired holdings to anyone else through gift, trade, sale, or bequest and that a person has a property right in whatever he receives in any of these ways so long as the person from whom he received it had a property right in whatever he transferred. To summarize: the right to property Nozick endorses is the right to exclusive control over anything one can get through initial acquisition (subject to the proviso) or through voluntary exchanges with others who have a property right in what they transfer.

An overall distribution of holdings, then, is just if and only if it actually arose from a previous just distribution by just means. But since, as Nozick acknowledges, not all existing holdings arose through just processes (that is, actions that satisfy the Principle of Just Initial Acquisition and the Principle of Just Transfers), a third principle, a Principle of Rectification of Past Injustices, is also needed.

If we set aside the special case of rectifying past injustices, Nozick's theory prohibits, on moral grounds, all attempts to redistribute wealth either by abolishing the market altogether or by welfare programs that allow the market to function but interfere with the resulting distribution by taxing the better off and transferring the proceeds to the worse off.

Surprisingly, Nozick does not provide any systematic justification for the very broad, alleged moral right to private property upon which his case for the virtually unfettered market is based. For this reason, Thomas Nagel has called Nozick's theory "libertarianism without foundations."[13] For that matter, Nozick's predecessor Locke does no better—he simply states that the rights he endorses are self-evident or "plain to the least reflection" by any rational being. This simplistic defense ignores the fact that the rights in question are highly controversial.

However, Nozick does argue indirectly for his theory of property rights and hence for the market as the only system capable of respecting those rights, by attempting to refute theories which limit the right to property and assign a welfare or redistributive role to the state. The most famous and perhaps the most important of these indirect arguments purports to show that any principle of justice that prescribes a certain distributive end-state or specified pattern of holdings will require unacceptably frequent and severe disruptions of individuals' holdings in order to achieve and maintain that end-state or pattern.[14]

Nozick's support for this very general conclusion consists of an appeal to our moral intuitions about a vivid example of redistribution.

Suppose that at time T some distribution of holdings prescribed by the most plausible principle of distributive justice is achieved—call this distribution D. Suppose that the famous basketball player, Wilt Chamberlain, signs a contract stating that he is to receive $.25 of the price of each ticket to all of the home games in which he plays. Suppose that Chamberlain makes $250,000 from this arrangement. At time T^1, when Chamberlain receives his $250,000, we no longer have distribution D; instead we have distribution D^1. In assuming that distribution D was just we assumed that those who paid $.25 to Chamberlain had a property right in the resources they possessed at T. The new distribution at T^1 arose through strictly voluntary exchanges of just holdings. Surely we must agree, Nozick says, that the new distribution at T^1 (after Chamberlain has received $250,000) cannot be unjust. Nozick concludes that in order to prevent departures from a prescribed end-state or pattern of holdings it would be necessary to interfere in unwarranted ways in peoples' voluntary exchanges. He seems to think that these interferences would be not only severe and frequent, but also unjust independently of their disruptiveness.

Nozick's use of this example to defend his theory of property rights and the market system which that theory supports is open to several serious objections. First, although the example may show that maintaining rather precisely specified distributive patterns or end-states, including strict equality, would require unacceptably frequent and severe disruptions of people's lives, it does not show that. *all* distributive patterns or end-states suffer from this problem. In particular, a principle requiring that everyone is to be guaranteed a decent minimum of certain basic goods such as food and shelter need not require frequent severe interferences. Long-standing, publicized laws specifying tax obligations can be and in fact are used to secure funds for providing a core of welfare goods. Such an arrangement avoids the disruption that would result from *ad hoc* prohibitions of particular actions or unpredictable expropriations of individuals' holdings. Consequently, as Friederich Hayek has observed, not all redistributive programs, or in Nozick's terms not all attempts to achieve and maintain distributive patterns or end-states, are incompatible with the existence of that stable framework of expectations which is the essence of the "rule of law."[15]

In the face of this criticism Nozick might concede that continued satisfaction of an end-state or patterned principle need not require frequent and severe disruptions. Nonetheless, he could argue, the Chamberlain example shows that it is intuitively unjust to interfere, through taxation or otherwise, with the results that arise then people voluntarily exchange what they have a right to according to some initially just distributive end-state or pattern. For if people only voluntarily exchange what they have a right to, how could anyone have a right to interfere with the resulting distribution?

Though his reasoning is far from clear here, Nozick may be assuming that it is permissible to interfere with a particular action only if that action, *considered in isolation*, is morally wrong or otherwise defective. This assumption, however, is very implausible, since it ignores something that is surely relevant from the standpoint of distributive justice in particular and the justification of interferences with liberty in general: the fact that a group of actions, none of which is criticizable in isolation, may *collectively* or *cumulatively* have unacceptable results. In effect, Nozick either ignores the existence of negative externalities and public goods problems, or assumes, without argument, the very unpersuasive thesis that the need to avoid negative externalities or to solve public goods problems can *never* provide a sound justification for interfering with the liberty to perform actions which, considered in isolation, are innocuous.

To make this fundamental point more concrete let us return to Nozick's example. Suppose that over an extended period of time voluntary exchanges of the sort Nozick describes in the Chamberlain case have the following extremely unfortunate result: a certain individual (or small group of individuals) comes to control a very large proportion of society's wealth and is able to use this financial power to gain a disproportionate share of political power, either through legal or illegal means.[16] (This, of course, is precisely what most socialist critics claim has in fact happened in all countries in which the market is largely unrestricted.) Considered in isolation, none of the voluntary exchanges which collectively produced this unacceptable result was itself criticizable in any way. But even if this is so, it does not follow that it would be wrong to prevent this extremely undesirable cumulative result by interfering with such exchanges—either by prohibiting them or by taxing the wealth of those who gain the most from them. Such interferences with liberty may be necessary to prevent concentrations of wealth and hence of power that would be even more detrimental to liberty. To assume that the cumulative result of a series of just actions must itself be just is to commit the fallacy of composition.

Nozick might reply that the only acceptable way to avoid undesirable cumulative results of actions that are just when considered in isolation is through *voluntary* abstention from the acts in question (that is, people agree in advance to refrain from certain harm-producing actions). This reply, however, is weak for two reasons. First, the unacceptable cumulative result may not be predictable in advance and the only remedy may be to deal with the problem after it is too late to refrain from the actions that gave rise to it. Second, and more importantly, this reply overlooks the fact that abstention from cumulatively harmful acts will often be a public good, subject to both the free-rider and assurance problems. In other words, even if each of us can predict in advance that the cumulative result of a group of voluntary exchanges over time will be disastrous for us all, each individual may nonetheless rationally conclude that he ought to engage in such transactions, either because he lacks assurance that enough others will abstain to prevent the cumulative harm or because he wishes to take a free ride on the abstention of others.

Finally, Nozick's use of the Chamberlain example to try to refute all end-state or patterned principles that would abolish or interfere with the market is subject to another related objection. This is because the people making the transactions are not the only ones affected by them. John Rawls and others have suggested that even if we set aside the problem of undesirable cumulative effects on those who engage in voluntary exchanges, we must contend with the possibility that such exchanges may result in unjust interferences with the liberty or equality of opportunity of the *offspring* of the parties involved. Rawls recognizes that one's social starting place—the social class and type of family one is born into—exerts a profound and pervasive influence upon one's opportunities throughout life, even though one clearly does not deserve and is in no way responsible for one's social starting point any more than for one's natural endowment. Rawls then argues that, at least if we value individual autonomy, we must commit ourselves to institutions that redress or at least partly compensate for these restrictions on opportunity, and hence upon individual autonomy, which are so "arbitrary from a moral point of view."[17] Rawls's general point can be rephrased in the light of our earlier criticism of Nozick as follows. Even if it were impermissible to interfere with exchanges which would be just in isolation for the sake of avoiding cumulative harms to those who voluntarily engage in the exchanges, it is nevertheless sometimes permissible and even obligatory to interfere in order to prevent serious limitations on the liberty or opportunities of those whose social starting positions will be strongly influenced by the cumulative effects of transactions in which they did not even participate.

The general force of this argument does not depend upon the assumption that *equality* of opportunity (or *equal* liberty), in any strict sense, is either a practical goal or a requirement of justice. All the argument requires is the much weaker and more plausible assumption that justice demands that *some limitations* be placed on the range of inequalities in social starting points that may arise as the cumulative result of voluntary exchanges in the market. At this point, those who find this latter assumption intuitively plausible will simply deny Nozick's premise that all interferences with the results of voluntary exchanges of holdings that were acquired in just ways are unjust.

Libertarians in general, including Nozick, often attempt to meet this line of criticism by invoking two distinctions. The first is a distinction between what is unjust, on the one hand, and what is merely unfair or morally unfortunate, on the other. While it may be morally unfortunate or even unfair that voluntary exchanges in the market lead to grossly unequal social starting points, it is not unjust. There is no valid principle of justice which authorizes the state or anyone else to use taxes or other forms of coercion to remedy the situation. For a situaiton can be unfair or morally unfortunate— though not unjust—so long as no individuals' *rights* were violated in bringing it about. It may be unfair or morally unfortunate that some individuals' opportunities or liberties are severely limited, or that some individuals perish from want of basic necessities as a result of market transactions that occurred before their birth, but this is not an injustice because individuals only have a right to noninterference with what is their property. No one has a right to positive aid (unless someone voluntarily grants such a right to him).

The second distinction the libertarian invokes is between the re-quirements of justice and the duties of charity or beneficence. Nozick and other libertarians are quick to observe that a libertarian theory of justice, which is limited to principles prohibiting violations of individuals' rights, is only one part of a comprehensive libertarian moral theory. Such a theory will also contain a theory of virtues, including principles stating the moral duty to be charitable to the needy. According to the libertarian, the key difference between the requirements of justice and the duty of charity is that the former may be coercively enforced while the latter is voluntary. So even if strict adherence to the principles of justice would result in an unfettered market system that might well produce severe deprivation or loss of opportunities for millions, the problem can be alleviated through purely voluntary beneficence. Although justice demands that no one shall be forced to contribute to the well-being of others, the duty of charity requires that those who are better off should help those in need, even though the latter have no *right* to aid. The cumulative effects of market transactions may in fact create unequal starting places that constitute awesome limitations on some individuals' liberties and opportunities, and charity may require that something be done to ameliorate this morally unfortunate or unfair situation. But since the market processes from which these inequalities arose violated no one's rights, justice does not require or even permit *enforced* redistribution.

This libertarian rejoinder is far from convincing as it stands because it appears to beg the question as to what is a matter of justice and what is a matter of charity. The libertarian assumes without argument that the nature and scope of individual rights, and hence of the requirements of justice, can be specified *independently* of considering the need to prevent extremely undesirable cumulative effects of actions which in isolation appear to violate no one's rights. Once we agree that the principles specifying individuals' rights are not self-evident truths, we may conclude that various considerations, including the need to prevent serious losses of political liberty or opportunity as cumulative effects of market exchanges, ought to be taken into account in determining what rights individuals have or in demarcating the *scope and limits* of those rights. While this reply may not show conclusively that the libertarian has in fact begged the question, it does at least raise the issue of where the burden of proof lies in disputes over where the line is to be drawn between justice and charity. And in doing so it casts grave doubts on libertarian defenses of the market which assume that this distinction can be clearly and uncontroversially drawn and drawn in such a way as to rule out all coercively enforced redistribution or other interference with the market.

It is important to understand that even if the libertarian could adequately support his distinction between justice and charity and do so in such a way as to show that the negative cumulative effects of the market on liberty and opportunity are not injustices because they violate no one's rights, it would still not follow *from this alone* that coercive interference with the market is unjustified. The latter conclusion would only follow if a further, quite questionable libertarian assumption is granted: that coercion is morally justified *only* if it is needed to prevent violations of individuals' rights. Here I shall only sketch a criticism of this key assumption that I have developed in greater detail elsewhere.[18]

Libertarians such as Nozick who stress that voluntary beneficence can ameliorate the harsh distributional effects of the unrestricted market tend to overlook two facts: first, that to be effective, voluntary beneficence often needs to be collective and coordinated rather than individual and uncoordinated; and second, that coordinated, collective beneficence can, like familiar public goods, be subject to both the free-rider and assurance problems.

Some of the most important forms of aid, especially those requiring large-scale investment for technology, cannot be provided through uncoordinated, individual acts of beneficence. Sophisticated medical services, as well as medical research, are clear examples of the need for coordinated, collective efforts. However, if beneficence is strictly a voluntary matter, these and other important forms of aid may not come about due to familiar barriers to collective action. Two related arguments for this conclusion can be distinguished.

The first argument shows that, in the absence of enforced obligations to contribute, the free-rider problem may block efforts at coordinated, collective beneficence. Suppose I am a genuinely beneficent individual. I realize that there are many ways in which I might help those in need. Since health is so important, coordinated, collective efforts to provide the needy with basic health services may be a very important form of beneficence, and indeed may be much more effective than any of the various uncoordinated individual acts of charity which I or others might perform. However, the rational individual will reason here, as in the case of public goods, as follows. Either a sufficient number of others will contribute to the collective effort to make it successful, even if I do not contribute to it; or not enough others will contribute, even if I do contribute. Granted the small size of my contribution and the fact that my making a contribution represents a definite cost in terms of lost opportunities to channel the same resources into alternative individual charitable acts whose success does not depend upon the contribution of others, the probability that my contribution to the collective effort would be decisive is negligible. But if this is true, then the rationally beneficent course for me is not to waste my contribution on the collective project but rather to undertake some independent act of beneficence whose success does not depend on the actions of others. However, if everyone (or a sufficient number of people) reason in this fashion, then the collective project, which we all agree is the most effective form of beneficence, will not succeed. It looks as if enforcement of the duty to contribute to the collective project may be needed here, as in more familiar cases of public goods.

The second argument begins in the same way but focuses on the assurance problem. Suppose again that I wish to be beneficent, desire to make my beneficence as effective as I can, and recognize that for some important forms of aid to the needy, coordinated, collective efforts are required. Suppose also that I am committed to contributing to such a collective project, but only if I can be assured that enough others will also contribute to achieve the threshold of investment needed for success. Though I have no desire to take a free ride on the efforts of others, I will nevertheless conclude that it would be irrational, and indeed morally irresponsible, to waste my resources on the collective project unless I have solid assurance that others will contribute to it as well. Lacking such assurance, the rationally beneficent course of action for me is to divert my resources to some independent act of beneficence, even though I know that such uncoordinated, independent efforts are not as effective. Again, if others reason as I do, then what we all agree to be the most effective way to help the needy will not come about. Each of us may reason that others may not contribute either because their sense of beneficence is submerged by their self-interest or because they reason as I did in the first argument, or because they suspect that others will take a free ride. And as in the first argument, it may be that enforced contribution is the only way to make beneficence effective.

Notice that the two arguments are really distinct. In the second argument the individual's reason for not contributing is simply that he lacks assurance that others will contribute. In the first argument, the individual concludes that he should not contribute even if he were assured that others would contribute. Yet in neither argument is it assumed that the barrier to successful collective action is egoism or self-interest in any significant sense. Instead, the laudable desire to be effectively beneficent may be self-defeating, where coercion is absent. So even in a society of morally upright, altruistic libertarians, the impulse to collective beneficence may be impotent.

There is at least one strategy which might be thought to solve the problem by providing a rebuttal of both arguments. Suppose arrangements were made so that each beneficent individual could contribute to the joint charitable venture with the assurance that if the target goal were not reached his contribution would be refunded, minus a share of the administrative costs, and that if the target goal were exceeded he would be refunded a portion of the excess, again minus administrative costs.[19] Would not the rationally beneficent individual— the person who wants the most beneficence bang for his bucks, so to speak—contribute to the joint venture?

Whether or not the refund strategy would solve the problem of collective charitable action in any particular case depends upon several factors, including the magnitude of the administrative costs and time costs of the scheme and the interest rate. If the administrative costs of the refund scheme were great, if the refund procedure was rather time-consuming and if the interest rate were sufficiently high, then the rationally beneficent thing to do might be to refrain from contributing to such a scheme and to engage instead in an individual act of beneficence. In other words, if such a scheme were likely to tie up one's beneficence budget for a period of time in which that budget could be expanding by earning interest, one might conclude that there were more effective uses for those resources.

The two arguments sketched earlier only show that there are prima facie obstacles to collective charitable action. The refund strategy provides a reply that may be adequate under certain conditions. Whether or not the obstacles to collective charitable action can be .overcome appears to admit of no general answer. It would be a mistake to conclude either that these obstacles can always be surmounted or that they never can.

Both of the arguments for enforced beneficence presented thus far proceed on the assumption that the individuals in question are motivated by a desire *to be* charitable, not simply by a desire *that the needy be provided for* (by someone or other). In our world, however, some people are more concerned about the latter than the former. Some may derive satisfaction or avoid discomfort simply by knowing that the needy are provided for. Others may view aid to the needy as instrumentally good: it makes for a more stable structure in which those who have wealth and power may enjoy them in greater security.

If an individual's goal is simply the provision of aid to the needy, then he may withhold his contribution if he believes that the needy will be provided for or that they will not, through the contribution of others, regardless of whether he contributes. So if a sufficient number of individuals are motivated primarily by the desire that charity be done rather than by a desire to be charitable, efforts for collective beneficence may succumb to the free rider problem in its classic form. This result is not especially surprising. What is surprising is the more general conclusion, which the three arguments for enforced beneficence together establish, namely that strictly voluntary efforts for collective charity may fail regardless of whether people are motivated chiefly by a desire to be charitable or by a desire that charity be done.

As we saw earlier in our discussion of the relationship between externalities and public goods problems, a standard and widely accepted response to problems of collective action is to employ a coercive mechanism, usually the government, to attach penalties to noncontribution. By enforcing the duty to contribute, government supplies each individual both with an assurance that enough others will contribute so that his contribution will not be wasted and with an incentive to contribute even if he suspects that enough others will contribute to achieve success without his contribution. I suggest that this widely accepted form of argument provides at least a prima facie justification for enforced contribution, and hence for coercive interference with the results which the unfettered market would produce, *even if no individual has a moral right to aid.* If there are *any* instances in which these arguments succeed (either for enforced beneficence or for enforced contributions to public goods), then it follows that we must reject the libertarian assumption that coercion is justified only if it is needed to prevent violations of individuals' right and we must also abandon all arguments for the unrestricted market, including Nozick's, that rest on this assumption. For none of these arguments for enforced contribution depends upon the assumption that individuals have a moral right to beneficence or to the public goods in question.

It is not difficult to see why the libertarian might mistakenly think it is virtually self-evident that coerced contributions are justified only if someone has a right to the good in question. For the libertarian may reason as follows. Everyone has a basic moral right against coercion (that is, a right to negative liberty). The only thing morally weighty enough to justify infringement of this right against coercion would be another moral right. Therefore, if enforced contribution (to collective goods) is ever morally justified, then its justification presupposes that individuals have a moral right to the good in question.

My criticism of this libertarian view is straightforward. The claim that there is a general moral right against coercion (or to negative liberty) strong enough to rule out all enforced contribution to collective goods is nonquestion-begging only if the right in question is viewed as a presumptive moral claim, (that is, a prima facie right) rather than as a justified moral claim (that is, a right, all things considered). In other words, if the libertarian supports his premise that there is such a strong right against coercion (or to negative liberty) merely by an appeal to our moral intuitions, but views the right as a justified moral claim rather than as a prima facie right or moral presumption, he begs the question against the nonlibertarian. For the nonlibertarian can simply point out that his moral intuition is that a virtually unlimited moral right against coercion is simply too unlimited a right to be plausible. In other words, the nonlibertarian can say that though he finds a strong presumption against interference to be intuitively plausible, he does not find intuitively plausible the much stronger claim that there is a moral right against coercion, if this latter claim entails that the only thing morally weighty enough to justify coercion is a moral right. Yet if the libertarian admits that an appeal to our moral intuitions only supports a prima facie general moral right against coercion, then he cannot assume that the *only* consideration morally weighty enough to defeat this presumption would be a moral right (to receive some good).

Indeed the nonlibertarian can even admit that there is a right against coercion (not just a prima facie right) but that so far as the existence of this right can be supported adequately by an appeal to noncontroversial intuitions, its scope and content are not sharply specified. He can then argue that when it comes to specifying the scope and content of this right, one morally relevant consideration is the need to overcome barriers to successful collective action for providing certain morally important goods or for preventing certain morally important harms. Once the proper content and scope of the right against coercion have been determined, it may *then* be correct to say, with respect to the *specified* right, that only another basic moral right could justify its infringement. What the libertarian overlooks is the possibility that in moving from the intuitively plausible assumption that there is a prima facie right to negative liberty or against coercion to a specification of the scope and limits of that moral right, nonrights-based considerations—including the need to use coercion to secure certain important collective goods—may be legitimate.

In sum, the libertarian's premise that there is a general moral right to negative liberty (that is, against coercion) may be understood either as a claim about a prima facie right or as a claim about a right *simpliciter*, a right all things considered. If the former, then the premise is intuitively plausible, but it does not follow that the only thing morally weighty enough to override the (merely prima facie) claim to negative liberty (against coercion) is a moral right. If the latter, then it may be true that only a moral right would be weighty enough to override the (justified) claim to negative liberty or against coercion, but the premise that there is a right to negative liberty or against coercion which is broad enough to rule out all arguments for enforced contribution is not something which the libertarian can support simply by an appeal to intuition. It appears, then, that the libertarian cannot support his assumption that coerced contribution is justified only when there is a right to the good in question by an intuitive appeal to a right to negative liberty or against coercion. To admit that some enforced principles requiring contributions to public goods or to coordinated, collective beneficence are morally justifiable (even in the absence of a moral right to the goods in question) is not, however, to say that whenever a problem of collective action exists, enforcement is justified. First of all, since enforcement, even if not always a great evil, is never a good thing, the need to overcome the free-rider or assurance problems generates enforceable principles only if the good cannot be attained by other, less-undesirable means (for instance, moral exhortation and leading others to contribute by one's example). Second, and perhaps even more obviously, enforcement is not justified if the cost of enforcement surpasses the benefit of attaining the good in question. Third, even when the preceding two conditions are satisfied, further limitations may be needed to restrict the scope of public goods arguments for enforcement, simply because the class of things which can qualify as public goods is so extremely large that overuse of this type of argument for enforcement may result.

A libertarian might raise the objection that such nonrights-based arguments for enforced contributions (and hence for interferences with market distributions) fail to recognize a fundamental qualification. While acknowledging that there may be some rules of social coordination or some principles specifying obligations to contribute to important public goods that rational individuals would wish to see enforced, even in the absence of corresponding rights, the libertarian will point out that enforcing them is permissible *only if* enforcement does not itself violate important moral rights.

I agree with this qualification. However, if the qualification is to become a sound criticism either of public goods arguments or of the "enforced beneficence" arguments just set out, the libertarian must discharge two difficult tasks, the second of which no one has yet achieved. First, he must clearly specify *which* basic moral rights would be violated by any attempt to enforce duties to contribute to important public goods or to enforce duties of beneficence, even the relatively undemanding duty to contribute to a collective effort to provide a decent minimum of goods and services for those who cannot provide for themselves. Second, he must provide a coherent and plausible *justification* for the claim that these basic moral rights do exist. To rule out in principle all enforceable principles requiring contribution to public goods and all enforceable principles of beneficence, the libertarian would have to specify and justify either a virtually unlimited general right of negative liberty (or against coercion) or a virtually unlimited right to private property. The great obstacle to doing either, as I noted earlier, is that he must do so without begging the question by appealing to intuitions that his nonlibertarian opponent does not share. In the absence of a sound theoretical justification for such rights, the burden of proof is on the libertarian to substantiate the claim that *every* such nonrights-based argument for enforced contribution violates important moral rights.

On the other hand, one might draw quite a different, and in some ways, more radical conclusion from these reflections on the need for enforced contribution, either for important public goods or for coordinated, collective beneficence. One might retain the libertarian's assumption that coercion is justified only when needed to prevent violations of individuals' rights, but reject the assumption that individuals only have rights to noninterference or negative liberty and have no rights to aid. In other words, some who are impressed with the obstacles to voluntary provision of certain public goods or to voluntary, coordinated, collective beneficence may conclude that the line between rights and charity should be redrawn so as to include some rights to receive aid, or that the most plausible theory of rights will include rights to certain public goods.[20] Regardless of which conclusion is drawn, these arguments present at least a serious challenge to libertarian attempts to show that coercive redistribution of what the market yields, or more direct coercive interferences with the market, are *never* morally justified (except to rectify past violations of libertarian negative rights).

The Argument from Liberty

Perhaps the most common argument in favor of the market, on grounds other than efficiency, is the contention that the market provides the best protection for civil and political liberties. The chief idea is that because the market requires a minimum of concentrated, coercive power, it minimizes the most dangerous threat to those especially valuable liberties that are enshrined as constitutional rights in the Western democracies. More generally, it is claimed that in addition to minimizing concentrated political power, the market disperses power generally. At least where there is competition, a person can escape one individual's or group's noxious exercise of power by dealing with someone else.

Some defenders of the market have gone so far as to argue that the impersonal nature of interpersonal relations in the market is, at least in the long run, a person's best protection against the detrimental effects of racist or sexist discrimination, religious persecution, or simple unpopularity.[21] A competitor who allows such personal likes and dislikes to influence his economic choices in the market, so the argument goes, will eventually be driven out by competition. Both versions of the argument from liberty assume that liberty is preeminently valuable: as something which all or most people find instrinsically satisfying, or as a necessary condition for successfully pursuing other ends they happen to have, or as something which facilitates the rational choosing of ends.

 The Market as the Best Protector of Civil and Political Liberties Some of the most ardent advocates of the market advance an extreme and unqualified version of the claim that that system provides the best protection of civil and political liberties.[22] They strongly suggest, when they do not explicitly state, that any departure from a virtually unfettered market system is unacceptably dangerous to civil and political liberties. It is essential to notice that this is an empirical prediction—and an extraordinarily sweeping one.

Moreover, there is considerable empirical data which tends to disconfirm it. As has often been observed, severe infringements of civil and political liberties have occurred in societies in which the market played a very prominent role (as in the case of violations of the civil and political rights of blacks in the United States). Similarly, some societies (such as the Scandinavian countries) have interfered significantly with the market while preserving a rather commendable record on civil and political liberties. It will do no good to protest that economic liberties are significantly curtailed in the latter societies, since what is at issue is the strength of the correlation between interferences with the market (which necessarily involve restrictions on economic liberties) and infringements of civil and political liberties. At best, contemporary and historical evidence supports the much more guarded empirical hypothesis that in societies in which the state is extremely powerful and the scope of the market is either nil or very small, civil and political liberties have suffered. So at least at present, the argument from civil and political liberties is not capable of supporting the case for a virtually unfettered market.

Further, it is extremely difficult to support more specific empirical predictions as to just when interferences with the market will reach the threshold of serious danger to civil and political liberties. This is due to the fact that the threshold will surely be a function of many factors, including the particular cultural, social, and political history of the country in question. At most the argument from civil and political liberties provides a very general prima facie case for minimizing interferences with the market, but one whose strength will vary greatly depending upon the nature of the interference in question and the social and historical context in which it is to occur.

The Market and Liberty in General   There is a second version of the argument, which claims that a market system is best because there is a strong correlation between the existence of markets and the flourishing of individual liberty in general, not just civil and political liberty. It is, however, equally implausible if construed as an argument for a virtually unrestricted market, and for the same reason: the sweeping empirical generalization on which it rests is subject to too many counterexamples. In addition, the second, more general version of the argument from liberty falls prey to other objections. As socialists have long been quick to observe, a system in which personal and governmental power is dispersed may nonetheless produce severe interferences with individual liberty or opportunity. In criticizing libertarian defenses of the market we saw that the cumulative effects of particular actions which do not themselves involve deliberate interference and which do not require concentrations of power can nevertheless impose severe limitations upon individual freedom and opportunity. Now if we simply define 'coercion' (as some libertarians do) as deliberate interference with liberty, then it will follow that the market system, which does disperse power when competition is strong, will provide greater opportunities for the individual to escape *coercive* (that is, deliberate) interferences with liberty. But it does not follow that such a system minimizes restrictions on liberty or opportunity in general, including those "noncoercive" restrictions which emerge as the cumulative results of multitudes of actions which are not themselves cases of deliberate interference. It is a profound irony that those who defend the market by ignoring interferences with liberty and opportunity that are not themselves the deliberate acts of persons or governments have failed to assimilate the basic truth which Adam Smith and other early proponents of the market so clearly perceived— that deliberate actions can have results (undesirable as well as desirable) which no one foresaw or intended.

A more sophisticated and self-critical version of the general argument from liberty would frankly acknowledge either that there can be noncoercive restrictions on liberty or that coercion need not be deliberate, and then would go on to argue that the restrictions on liberty and opportunity that individuals face in the market are in general less debilitating than those which occur where the market is abandoned in favor of a thoroughgoing socialism. If by the latter is meant a form of social organization in which so much power is concentrated in the government that there is in effect only one employer, then this argument is quite powerful. For in such a society there will be no escape from persecution or discrimination, as there may be in a society in which competition for goods, services, and labor prevails. Once again, however, the argument provides only a strong case for preserving a large role for the market, not for a virtually unrestricted market system.

The Market, Private Property, and Individual Personality A related argument for the market relies on the premise that the system of private property which constitutes the core of an unrestricted market society is necessary for the fullest development of individual personality. The idea is that unless one is at liberty to use one's property as one sees fit, one cannot adequately develop either those general capacities for choice which are distinctive of persons nor that particular constellation of talents and interests which constitute one's uniqueness, one's individuality. In Hegel's version of this argument, the unfolding of individual personality requires that one be able to express oneself concretely by creating and modifying material things according to one's own aims and this in turn requires that others recognize one's property rights. Though Hegel himself makes it clear that he sees this as an argument for *private* property rights, this conclusion can certainly be challenged. Even if the expression and development of individual personality requires *personal* property, it does not follow that one must have *private* property if the latter includes exclusive control over the more important forms of the means of production.[23] But even if the argument could be filled out to support the stronger conclusion that exclusive control over some means of production (including the right to exchange them) is a necessary condition of the full development of individual personality, it would at best provide an argument for the existence of a market in *some* means of production, not for an unfettered market in all means of production.

In fact, once a strong connection is acknowledged between the development of individual personality and control over the means of production, the argument may take a turn toward the left. Marx and later socialists radicalized Hegel's argument by arguing that, at least in a society in which there is a relatively unfettered market in the most vital means of production, many people, perhaps the majority, will lack the material conditions for fully developing their individual personalities. It seems, then, that even if the argument supports the conclusion that not only personal property but also private property in the means of production is necessary, it falls far short of justifying the much more ambitious conclusion that significant restrictions on the market are incompatible with the full development of individual personality.

The Argument from the Conditions for the Effective Exercise of Basic Rights

This moral argument *against* the market arises in response to the contention, encountered earlier, that the market is the surest safeguard of civil and political liberties. The latter position fails to distinguish between two quite different questions. (1) Does the market system provide the best protection of individual legal equal *rights* to political participation, to free speech, to legal due process, and so forth? (2) Is the market system compatible with keeping within acceptable limits *inequalities in individuals' abilities to exercise these equal rights effectively?* According to most socialist critics of the market, the answer to the second question is no, even if the answer to the first is yes.

The argument depends upon a distinction between merely having an equal legal right to something and having the resources to be able to exercise that right effectively in protecting one's interests or pursuing one's goals. To have an equal legal right to free speech, for example, is to be protected, by the coercive power of the state, in certain of one's expressive activities, from certain sorts of interferences. However, even where this legal right is impartially and effectively enforced for all, there may be enormous inequalities in the effectiveness with which different individuals can exercise it, due to inequalities in wealth and education that, at least in part, are due to market processes.

Consider the case of the right to free speech or the right to political participation, including the right to run for office. Some individuals are wealthy enough to purchase access to extremely expensive mass media. The vast majority are not. Those candidates who happen to own television stations have something of an advantage over those who cannot even afford television sets.

Inequality in access to mass media is only one example of the more pervasive problems of inequalities in the effectiveness of the exercise of equal legal rights to free speech and political participation. Inadequate nutrition and health care, aggravated by cultural deprivation and the substandard public education often found in poorer neighborhoods, can contribute to gross discrepancies in the effectiveness of these and other equal, legal rights.

Palpable inequalities in wealth, education, and access to health care contribute to sharp differences in the effectiveness with which individuals can exercise the equal right of legal due process as well. There is more than a grain of truth in the cynical slogan that capital punishment means you can avoid the punishment if you have the capital. Even if we bracket the undeniable role of poverty as at least one of the factors that gives rise to crime, numerous studies purport to show that poor people who are arrested for crimes are more likely to be prosecuted, more likely to be convicted, and often draw stiffer sentences than their more affluent counterparts.[24] Finally, people who are poor and uneducated are often less effectively protected by the law and are less likely in many cases to receive adequate compensation or restitution if they become the victims of crimes. In the civil law the disparity between equal rights and unequal effectiveness in their exercise may be just as great. In both areas of the law better-educated and more affluent people are generally better able to secure good legal advice and effective professional representation of their interests, at least where the market operates freely and where there are no public subsidies to aid those who are less fortunate.

It is important to see that those who criticize the market in this way need not be guilty of making either of two mistakes. In order to argue for interventions in the market to narrow the range of inequalities in the effectiveness of equal basic rights, one need not make either the error of assuming that (a) *strictly equal* effectiveness is feasible or desirable, or the error of assuming that (b) the mere fact that someone has an equal right to something *entails* that he has a right to whatever is necessary for being able to exercise that right effectively.

Proponents of the argument can agree that the goal of strictly equal effectiveness in the exercise of equal rights would be impossible to achieve and that any serious attempt to attain strict equality would require intolerable infringements of individual liberty. (For one thing, differences in the effectiveness with which different persons can exercise equal rights in the pursuit of their goals will depend not only upon their wealth and education, but also upon effort, character traits, luck, personal attractiveness and, of course, the nature of those goals!) At most the argument supports the more modest conclusion that redistributive measures of one sort or another should be undertaken in order to impose *some limits* on the range of inequalities in the effectiveness of the exercise of equal rights.

Even more important, in its more plausible forms, the argument does *not* assume that one has a right to whatever one needs to exercise one's rights effectively. Instead, the simple and quite plausible idea is that the same moral and prudential considerations which lead us to regard equal legal rights as being important in the first place also count in favor of at least attempting to minimize the grosser inequalities in the effectiveness with which they can be exercised. After all, the value of equal legal rights lies in what one can *do* with them rather than in the mere satisfaction of knowing that one *has* them.[25] This is not to say, of course, that being greatly disadvantaged in one's ability to exercise one's equal legal rights is just as bad as not having equal rights at all; but it is to say that all the familiar arguments in favor of equal legal rights also lend support to the conclusion that controllable inequalities in their exercise should not be too great.

A second variant of the argument from effective rights uses the notion of *fair institutional procedures* to forge the needed link between recognizing equal rights and adopting measures to constrain the grosser discrepancies in the ability to exercise those rights effectively. The argument from fair institutional procedures, which I have developed at length elsewhere, can be briefly summarized as follows.[26] To concentrate only on ensuring that all have equal legal rights is to view the individual's possession of equal rights as an unalloyed benefit for that individual. This, however, is a serious mistake. The institutions that establish and enforce equal rights constitute a *monopolistic* or *exclusive* set of procedures. They determine not only how one may protect and pursue one's interests but also, on pain of punishment, how one may *not* do so. In other words, the system of enforced equal legal rights imposes stringent restrictions on the means by which a person may attempt to protect and pursue his interests when they conflict with those of others. Because the legal system prohibits many other forms of conflict-resolution, it places the individual in awesome dependence upon its distinctive procedures.

Once again, a concrete example will be helpful. Suppose a poor, uneducated person loses his meager property through fraud or theft. Because he is poor, he is unable to afford competent legal representation; because he is uneducated, he is ignorant of his legal rights. The system of enforced legal rights prohibits him from protecting his interests in extralegal ways even though the protections that system provides are ineffective for him. Surely it is fair to demand his compliance with the system, and to impose penalties on him if he fails to comply, only if he is assured that these procedures for conflict-resolution do not systematically disadvantage him in disastrous ways. Like the first version of the argument from effective rights, the argument from fair institutional procedures avoids both the error of assuming that strictly equal effectiveness is obligatory or even possible and the error of assuming that having a right to something entails having a right to whatever is necessary for exercising that right effectively.

Notice that neither variant of the argument from effective rights shows that the market should be abolished or even that a more egalitarian basic distribution of wealth and income is required to avoid intolerable inequalities in the effectiveness of the exercise of equal legal rights. For nothing has been said so far about *how* we should go about attempting to limit these inequalities. The strategies could range from providing publicly subsidized legal representation and publicly subsidized access to mass media, on the one hand, to a large-scale redistribution of wealth and income, on the other. Which of these approaches would be both effective and morally acceptable will depend upon their impact upon liberty and efficiency. Indeed, what counts as a tolerable range of inequalities in the effectiveness of equal rights will also depend in part upon the "costs," in terms of liberty and efficiency, of efforts to achieve equality of effectiveness. What the two arguments from the conditions for effective rights do show, however, is that something must be done to restrict the range of inequalities, and this surely requires some interferences with the distribution which the unfettered market system would yield.

At this point economists find it useful to distinguish between two broad forms which intervention might take. On the one hand, we

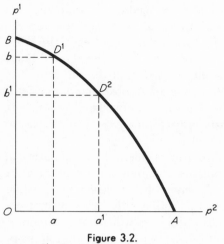

Figure 3.2.
The Pareto Optimality Frontier

might try to limit inequalities in the effectiveness of equal rights by interfering directly with the market processes in which individuals use their resources, without tampering with the initial distribution of resources they bring to the market or the incomes that result from market processes. On the other hand, we might redistribute rights to resources (property rights) and then allow the market to function without interference, or, more likely, we might redistribute income resulting from unimpeded market processes. So far our analysis has concentrated only on the First Fundamental Theorem of Welfare Economics, which states that the equilibrium state of the ideal market is Pareto Optimal. The Second Fundamental Theorem of Welfare Economics provides support for the second form of intervention. It states that, given an appropriate distribution (or redistribution) of property rights to resources, or an appropriate distribution (or redistribution) of income, *any* Pareto Optimal outcome can be achieved as the equilibrium of the ideal market.

The point to be emphasized is that there is no *unique* Pareto Optimal equilibrium state, as shown by Figure 3.2, which for simplicity represents a two-person, pure exchange economy, with a fixed stock of goods.

Point O, the origin, stands for the position prior to the distribution of goods between persons P^1 and P^2. All points along line AB represent Pareto Optimal distributions. If P^1 receives goods at quantity a, then the most goods P^2 can receive will be quantity b, and so on.

Distribution D^2 is more egalitarian than distribution D^1, but both are Pareto Optimal, as are all points on line AB. Suppose that a more from D^1 to D^2 would reduce inequalities in the effectiveness of certain basic rights for persons P^1 and P^2. The Second Fundamental Theorem of Welfare Economics tells us that distribution D^2 can be achieved as an equilibrium outcome of unobstructed market processes (granted that the conditions for the ideal market are satisfied), if we redistribute property rights to resources in an appropriate way or if we redistribute income appropriately.

This response to the problem of inequalities in the effectiveness of rights is only one instance of a more general strategy for attempting to preserve the efficiency of the ideal market while at the same time achieving fairness or justice. The idea is that we can ensure that unobstructed market processes will achieve outcomes that satisfy whichever conception of fairness or justice is most appropriate by a carefully tailored redistribution of property rights or by artfully designed lump-sum income transfers through taxation. Thus a substantial role for the market can be preserved without excessive moral costs.

Notice, however, that such a proposal, even as described by its proponents, does involve large-scale interference with the market. More precisely, it purports to interfere with the market as a distributive mechanism while not interfering with it as a mechanism for allocation of productive resources and for the organization of production. However, as critics of this approach have long pointed out, it may be very difficult if not impossible to modify property rights or incomes through taxation or through other means to achieve the desired distributional outcome without undermining incentives for productivity. In particular, the income tax, as a device to achieve the desired combination of efficiency and justice or fairness, has been far from successful. The point of this objection is that the nature of the incentives in a market system make it very difficult if not impossible to treat the distributive function of the market as if it were independent of the allocative and productive functions.

There is another, quite distinct problem with the strategy of relying on redistribution of property rights or income transfers to rebut the objection that the market produces unacceptable inequalities. Interestingly enough, this objection is advanced both by leftist critics of the market and by individuals at the opposite extreme of the ideological spectrum. It is the charge that the redistributive strategy, though sound *in principle* (as the Second Fundamental Principle of Welfare Economics shows), is not likely to succeed in practice because it overlooks the importance of *power relations*.

Critics on the left, beginning with Marx, argue that those who enjoy a disproportionate share of economic wealth tend to dominate the political process, and that they are not likely to use their political power to undermine their own position of superiority. According to other critics, who have little else in common with the left, the problem again is power, but the power of bureaucracies or of the worse off, not of the wealthy, to pursue their own possibly distorted ideals of justice or equality at the expense of efficiency. What both groups of critics point out is the yawning gap between the theoretical grounding of the redistributive strategy in the Second Fundamental Theorem of Welfare Economics and the justification of the statement that what is in theory possible can be achieved in practice.

The Argument from Exploitation

Exploitation of Workers by Capitalists and the Generally Exploitive Character of Interpersonal Relations in the Market Some of the most uncompromising critics of the market, including Marx and others in the socialist and communist traditions, condemn the market system as exploitive. The most specific version of this charge is that employers (capitalists) in the market system exploit their employees (workers). The more general version is that the market encourages a wide range of exploitive relations, including, but not restricted to, those between employers and workers. Those who advance the more general charge say, for example, that the existence of a market for ordinary commodities encourages the development of a market for sexual services, and thus contributes to the exploitation of women, directly, in the form of prostitution, and indirectly, in the form of what Marx described as the veiled prostitution of "bourgeois marriage."

Alternative Conceptions of Exploitation In spite of the popularity of arguments against the market system based on the notion of exploitation, there is a good deal of confusion and controversy as to what exploitation is. Here I will make no attempt to sort out all of the different conceptions of exploitation that are employed by various critics of the market. Instead I shall concentrate on two related notions that seem to be common to many if not all conceptions of exploitation. The first is the very general idea that to exploit a person involves the *harmful, merely instrumental utilization* of him or of his capacities, for one's own advantage or for the sake of one's own ends. The second conception of exploitation is that it involves a kind of *parasitism* or *lack of reciprocity*.[27]

According to the first view, to exploit a person is to treat him as if he were a mere tool, or an inanimate material resource to be expended for one's own advantage or ends, without regard to the harmful consequences for that person. Those who employ this conception of exploitation are often not clear as to whether the harm involved is only a *consequence* of merely instrumental utilization of persons and logically distinct from it, or whether treating a person as a mere instrument *itself constitutes* harming that person, apart from any harmful consequences that may arise. But regardless of whether or not the merely instrumental use of persons is intrinsically harmful to them, when the general conception of exploitation is applied to relationships in the market, the charge is that individuals harm one another by treating each other as mere instruments or means toward their own advantage.

Some libertarian defenders of the market object that so long as workers *voluntarily* make contracts with employers, and, more generally, so long as all exchanges are voluntary, no one is treated as a mere means or instrument. To *coerce* a person is to treat him as a mere means, but the voluntary exchanges made in the market are not coercive. Making exchanges conditional upon voluntary consent shows respect for persons as autonomous individuals and marks a clear distinction between them and mere tools or resources, which are incapable of giving consent.[28]

Some critics of the market, including some who condemn it for exploitation, reject the libertarian's claim that exchanges in the market are noncoercive because they reject the libertarian's restriction of "coercion" to physical force or the threat of physical force. They contend that workers, who lack control over the means of production which they must use if they are to secure a living, are coerced by economic necessity into accepting the capitalist's terms, even though the capitalist does not use physical force or the threat of physical force against them.

Perhaps the most serious objection to this antimarket reply is that even if coercion is not always restricted to physical force or the threat of physical force, it may be very difficult to formulate a broader conception of coercion which is not so all-inclusive as to become useless. If, for example, a particular wage offer counts as coercive simply because the alternative to accepting some wage offer or other is poverty or starvation, then either the concept of coercion has been stretched beyond credibility or the fact that a wage offer is coercive is not by itself sufficient to condemn it.

However, the criticism that market relations are exploitive need not depend upon the success of attempts to develop a concept of coercion which is both broad enough to rebut the libertarian's charge that market exchanges are not coercive and yet narrow enough to be plausible and morally significant. The critic of the market can instead concede the libertarian's narrow use of the term 'coercion' and then argue that not all exploitation is coercive. For surely one person can harmfully utilize another as a mere instrument or means without coercing him in the narrow, libertarian sense. Outside the economic sphere, we say, for example, that a man exploits a woman (or vice versa) by playing upon her loyalty in order to serve his own ends, without regard to the harm that may result to her. Yet to do this no physical force or threat of physical force may be required. And in some cases such actions may even take place with the consent of the victim. Moreover, this consent may be every bit as voluntary as it is in the case of one's consent to an exchange under the pressure of "economic necessity" in the market. This is just to say that the notion of consensual exploitation is not incoherent.[29] So even if it is conceded that market relations are noncoercive it can still be claimed that they are exploitive.

The critic of the market need not stake his argument upon the propriety of the notion of consensual exploitation, however, He can simply dispense with the term 'exploitation' and limit himself to the charge that the market encourages the harmful, merely instrumental utilization of persons and their abilities, and that this form of inter-action, at least when it becomes as pervasive as it is in an advanced market system, is unacceptable, whether it qualifies as exploitation or not.

Such a move, however, merely shifts the burden of the argument. The critic of the market must now face the issue raised earlier concerning the connection between using a person as a mere means and harming him. If the relationship is merely causal—if what is wrong with treating a person as a mere means is that doing so usually leads to harmful consequences—then the real issue seems to be the harm. The debate then moves from the question of whether the market system is exploitive to the question of whether the harms which result from market exchanges violate individuals' rights or, if we adopt a utilitarian perspective, whether the overall harms exceed overall benefits—difficult questions we explored earlier.[30]

Alternatively, if treating a person as a mere means is in itself harmful to that person or in some other way intrinsically wrong, then much more must be said about why this is so. In addition, a clear distinction must be drawn between treating someone as a means and treating someone as a *mere* means, since treating others as means is neither avoidable, nor intrinsically wrong, nor always productive of harmful results. (If I politely ask you what time it is, I am using you as a means for learning the time, but there seems to be nothing wrong with this.)

Exploitation and Parasitism   It was observed earlier that a second element common to many discussions of the exploitive character of market relations is the idea that they involve a kind of *parasitism* or *lack of reciprocity*. My suggestion is that this second idea may be viewed either as a way of clarifying the notion of wrongful, merely instrumental use or as a more helpful substitute for it in a theory of exploitation.

Marx and other leftist critics of the market emphasize that the capitalist, who is said to exploit the worker, gets something for nothing or reaps benefits from the worker's activity without bestowing corresponding benefits upon him. Indeed, Marx describes the capitalist as a vampire and as a werewolf—a deadly human parasite feeding on the lifeblood of his fellows.[31]

Now a parasite derives benefit from its host, and, unlike a member of a symbiotic relationship (usually) confers no benefit in return. Yet since the capitalist does give something to the worker in exchange for his labor, namely wages, how can it be said that he is a parasite?

It is tempting to suggest that the parastie simile is hyperbolic: the Marxist's point is not that the capitalist gives nothing in return, but that he gives too little—that workers do not receive full compensation for what they do. This way of putting the charge of exploitation, however, runs the risk of trivializing the Marxist's demand for an end to exploitation by reducing it to a plea for higher wages. It is quite clear that Marx and other radical critics of the market see exploitation as a much deeper problem, one whose solution requires scrapping the whole market system, not merely modifying it by raising wages. It would be misleading, then, to say that the charge of exploitation focuses upon a *distributive* defect of the market system or that exploitation is simply a particular form of distributive injustice.[32] But if the capitalist does give something in return and if the problem is not merely that wages are too low relative to what the capitalist gets out of the exchange, in what sense is the relationship nonreciprocal or parastic?

The answer, I believe, lies in the assumption that a parasite is *superfluous* to the normal functioning or well-being of the host organism, as well as harmful. On this interpretation, even though the capitalist gives something in return for what he gets from the worker, he is nonetheless unnecessary to the well-being of the individuals whom he hires. But how can this be? Is not the capitalist, who controls the means of production, necessary at least *within* the market system? As the Marxist emphasizes, the worker needs the capitalist in order to gain access to the means of production and hence to live.

Some Marxists might reply that the sort of capitalist who *merely owns* the means of production, the idle individual who is not an entrepreneur and who performs no managerial functions, is not necessary even within the market system. This individual is surely a parasite, a totally superfluous and nonproductive taker.

However, this way of rebutting the view that the capitalist is necessary, at least within the market system, at first appears to come at an exorbitant price. It seems to reduce the very broad claim that capitalists exploit workers to the much narrower claim that that minority of capitalists who perform neither managerial nor entrepreneurial functions exploit workers. Even if the idle capitalist were eliminable, this would only show that a very small subset of capitalists is superfluous within the market system. It would not show that entrepreneurial or managerial owners of private property in the means of production are parasites in the market system. To deny that the entrepreneur or the capital-owning manager plays a vital role in the market system is simply to be grossly ignorant of how coordination comes about in that system.[33]

The Marxist criticism that the capitalist is a parasite can be reformulated, however, in a more promising manner by distinguishing between different roles which a capitalist may play. Thus it has been said that even the capitalist who functions as an entrepreneur or manager is still, qua capitalist, a parasite, a noncontributor, even if he does make a contribution in his other roles as entrepreneur or manager. Qua capitalist, the only "action" the capitalist performs is to allow the means of production he owns to be used by workers (in exchange for the use of their labor power) or to allow his money to be used (in return for interest). Even if his entrepreneurial and managerial functions make a genuine contribution to production, they are quite distinct from what he does qua capitalist (that is, as an owner of the means of production) and both the entrepreneurial and the managerial functions can be and often are in practice separated from the distinctive role of capitalist. It is only because the coercive power of the state enforces his legal right of ownership over the means of production that it is necessary to get the capitalist to allow others to use his resources. So even if the capitalist qua entrepreneur or manager is a contributor, the capitalist qua capitalist makes no contribution to production. He is a pure parasite and this is the sense of the objection that the capitalist, that is, *every* capitalist qua capitalist, exploits the worker.[34]

The defender of capitalism, and of the market so far as it includes private property in the means of production, still has a strong reply. There are at least two independent arguments to show that the capitalist *qua* capitalist, and quite independently of any entrepreneurial or managerial contribution, is not superfluous.

The first, which has been explored in detail by Scott Arnold,[35] relies upon the most general version of the time preferences theory of interest. That theory contains two key propositions. (1) Capital formation, the accumulation of productive resources, requires that someone refrain from consuming some currently available goods. (2) Different individuals have different time preferences with respect to the consumption of goods. (For example, while A [the borrower] values *$10 now* more than he values *$10 + $1 interest six months from now,* B [the lender] values *$10 now* less than he values *$10 + $1 interest six months from now.*) If (2) is true, that is, if different individuals have different preferences for goods, then exchanges between them will occur, if each pursues his own interest. The situation here is precisely the same as in Adam Smith's pure barter exchange economy in which A trades 2 beaver pelts to B in return for 1 deer. The voluntary exchange is possible (and will occur if each party maximizes his own utility) because the 2 parties value the same goods differently. A values 1 deer more highly than he values 2 beaver pelts; B values 1 deer less highly than he values 2 beaver pelts. Similarly the exchange takes place between the capitalist and the worker or between the capitalist and the entrepreneur because they value the same goods differently. At this level of description, at least, the capitalist is not necessarily an exploiter—unless all voluntary exchanges are exploitive!

Granted differences in time preference for different individuals, the prospect of receiving interest, broadly construed as the return one gets for allowing others to use one's resources, serves as an effective motivation for forgoing current consumption, that is, for accumulating resources. So not only is the capitalist (qua capitalist) every bit as much a contributor as each party to any voluntary, mutually beneficial exchange, but also the profit (interest) the capitalist receives plays a vital motivational role in a system of exchange which allows individuals with different time preferences to satisfy those preferences in a mutually beneficial way, through voluntary agreements.

The second argument against the claim that the capitalist qua capitalist is superfluous is that this charge simply ignores one of the most important traditional justifications for private ownership of the means of production: the view that the chance to gain wealth, including sufficient wealth to allow one to delegate managerial and entrepreneurial tasks to others, provides a strong incentive for risk-taking, effort, and investment, and thereby increases productivity. In other words, even if the idle capitalist who merely clips bond coupons and performs no entrepreneurial or managerial tasks is not himself productive in any important sense, it does not follow that his "role" is eliminable within the system.

'Exploitation' as a Theoretical Term in Search of a Theory   We can now summarize the progress of the controversy thus far. The exploitation theorist who takes the Marxian parasite simile seriously contends that the capitalist qua capitalist (independently of entrepreneurial or managerial functions) is a noncontributing taker, a pure parasite. This charge seems unfounded, however, for at least two reasons. First, the role of capitalist is not nonfunctional insofar as the prospect of becoming wealthy enough to delegate managerial and entrepreneurial tasks to others motivates some people to perform more productively than they otherwise would. Second, assuming the main elements of the time preference theory of interest are correct, the capitalist (qua capitalist) is as productive as any party to any mutually beneficial, voluntary exchange. The capitalist, then, is not superfluous; he is a contributor to social welfare.

Those who hold that the capitalist qua capitalist exploits the worker have one final reply. Even if it is acknowledged that the capitalist qua capitalist is a contributor, and hence not a pure parasite strictly speaking, there is nonetheless an important sense in which he is superfluous. Even if the prospect of becoming an idle capitalist in fact does function as an incentive in the capitalist system, this is not the only way, nor necessarily the best way, to motivate people to be productive. In alternative social arrangements quite different incentives for productivity would operate. Further, the time preference argument is also inadequate to show that the role of capitalist is uneliminable, even if it shows that within the capitalist system the capitalist does contribute. As proponents of the time preference theory themselves point out, one virtue of that theory is that it provides an explanation of interest that is not limited to systems in which there is private property in the means of production. And as we shall see in chapter 4, various market socialism models include a role for interest (and hence for exchanges between individuals or groups with different time preferences) while eliminating the role of capitalist—that is, the individual owner of productive resources. These models typically assign the role of lender of productive resources to the central government. Finally, there is a sense in which the time preference theory as a defense of the role of capitalist does not go deep enough. Why is it that the capitalist has a different time preference from that of the entrepreneur or worker? The answer, of course, is that the capitalist possesses *greater wealth* than the other party to the exchange, more wealth than he would prefer to consume now, granted an opportunity to turn a profit in the future. While it is true that the capitalist does make a contribution in the exchange between himself and others with different time preferences, the major source of the difference in time preferences is the inequality of the system in which the exchanges occur. Hence if these inequalities in wealth are unjustified, and if they can be eliminated or reduced (without disproportionate moral costs or disproportionate losses in efficiency), then the fact that the capitalist is a contributor, not a pure parasite, is not an adequate defense of the system. His contribution is an artifact of defective distribution arrangements and will disappear when they are abolished.

A more charitable interpretation of the Marxist's parasite simile, then, is that capitalists in general are superfluous to the worker's well-being in the sense that the *role* of capitalist is only a necessary role in a *system* which is itself superfluous to the well-being of the worker, and harmful to him. In other words, even if the worker in the market system needs the capitalist, the worker does not need the market system. So on its most plausible interpretation, the claim that the capitalist is a parasite, an unproductive, unnecessary taker, rests upon the implicit assumption that there is a *feasible alternative system*, in which the role of capitalist is eliminated, but which will provide for the well-being of the workers.

Providing adequate support for this latter assumption, as difficult as this might be, would not by itself be sufficient to show that the capitalist exploits the worker or that the market system should be condemned. Unless it can also be shown that the alternative, nonmarket system avoids the harmful effects that are the price the worker must pay if he is to survive in the market system, the claim that the capitalist's role could be eliminated by the transition to an alternative system which lacks that role is rather uninteresting. For the same could be said about social roles in the alternative, nonmarket system! Those roles may also be superfluous in precisely the same sense: even though they are necessary roles in a socialist system, they could be eliminated if an alternative system, for example, a market system, were established instead. So the critic of the market who claims that the capitalist exploits the worker, as a debilitating parasite exploits his host, must show not only that there is a feasible alternative system in which the role of capitalist is unnecessary but also that this alternative system avoids the harms that befall workers in the market system while providing equal or greater benefits.

Those who charge that the market is exploitive, like the overwhelming majority of critics of the market, have in mind the market in its most familiar theoretical and historical form: the market with private property in the means of production. However, it is far from obvious that exploitation is limited to the market with private property in the means of production. The possibility that an individual will be exploited exists wherever some other individual or group controls the means of production, and this can occur in nonmarket systems as well as in market systems which lack private property in the means of production. (In the latter case the majority might exploit the minority.)

If the preceding analysis of the charge that a private property market system is exploitive is correct (where the charge is viewed as a radical condemnation, not simply as a complaint about low wages), then those who advance it are committed to two onerous tasks. First, they must either develop (a) a theory of nonmarket social organization, or (b) a theory of market organization *without* private ownership of the means of production, in sufficient detail to support judgments about how such a system would allocate resources and produce and distribute goods. Second, they must overcome the difficulties encountered earlier in making intersystemic efficiency comparisons in order to show that the alternative system would not only avoid the harms that befall individuals in the market system with private property but also would achieve equal or greater levels of productive and distributive efficiency. In other words, as a claim about parasitism or lack of reciprocity the charge that the private property market system is exploitive or that capitalists exploit workers is a theoretical statement, not a theory-neutral empirical claim. But so far it is a theoretical statement which is still in search of a theory. We have already noted the current unavailability of a explanatorily powerful theory of feasible nonmarket social organization. In the final chapter we shall explore an embryonic theory—the theory of market socialism—which separates the market from private property in the means of production.

The Argument from Alienation and the Concept of Positive Freedom

Main Elements of the Theory of Alienation   The market system is often condemned on the grounds that it breeds alienation. There is much disagreement, and often little clarity, as to what exactly 'alienation' means. Instead of attempting to canvass the whole range of conceptions of alienation, which extends from scholarly writings to casual observations on contemporary culture, I will focus on what I believe to be the most influential and important account—that found in the work of the greatest critic of capitalism, Karl Marx. While Marx's views on alienation borrow heavily from others, especially Hegel and Ludwig Feuerbach, the systematic critique of the market system as an alienating form of social organization is distinctively Marxian. For the purposes of this essay, a rather simplified sketch of the Marxian theory of alienation will do.[36]

That theory contains three chief elements. First, alienation is thought of as involving a human being's estrangement from, and lack of control over, his own products. This component of the Marxian theory of alienation is vividly captured in two well-known stories: the tale of the sorcerer's apprentice and that of Dr. Frankenstein's monster. In both, human intelligence, in an attempt to advance human knowledge and to extend the domain of human control over nature, produces something which takes on a life of its own and turns, destructively, against its creator. Similarly, the worker in capitalism periodically produces more goods than can be purchased, with the result that the system suffers "underconsumption crises." Capitalists in turn react by cutting back production—and they do this by laying off workers. In a sense, then, the worker's own creation, over which he exercises no control, dominates and harms him. More generally, Marx charges that worker and capitalist alike help to create a system of social institutions and social relations over which no one can exercise effective control and that in this broader sense the creation dominates the creator in the market system.

The Marxian theory of alienation then adds a new twist to the theme of the Frankenstein story. It is as if Dr. Frankenstein suffered from amnesia—he no longer recognizes that the uncontrollable monster threatening him is his own creation. The first element of the Marxian theory of alienation, in other words, is supplemented by a theory of *ideology* or *false consciousness*, which purports to explain how the social institutions and relations which human beings create serve to perpetuate the illusion that these institutions and relations are not human creations, subject to human control, but rather natural features of human life. Marx argues that while the market system and the egoistic, competitive mentality that go with it are artifices, human creations, those who live in that system tend to view them as unalterable features of the human condition.

The second chief element in the Marxian theory of alienation is the idea that alienation is, or at least involves, a lack of self-realization or of self-actualization. Though there is much dispute as to how the notion of the self is to be understood in this context, at least this much is relatively uncontroversial: the complaint is that the market system stunts individuals. It prevents them from developing the full range of their best capacities. In particular, it is said that the division of labor that is characteristic of the market system deprives individuals of the opportunity to become well-rounded beings who can freely choose to develop their talents. The worker lacks control not only over his product, but also over his productive activity. He is not free to engage in productive activities which he finds intrinsically satisfying or which stimulate his personal growth.

Critics of Marxism often condemn that view for its failure to give individuality its due. However, the Marxian concern about overcoming alienation can be seen as an affirmation of the importance of individuality, not a devaluation of it, if one thinks of the development of individual personality as a process in which the individual freely chooses to nurture and integrate a broad range of his talents into a whole which he regards as uniquely valuable and with which he identifies. And if it is conceded that there is a sense in which a human being creates his own distinctive "self," when he freely chooses which goals to pursue and which of his capacities to develop, then Marxian talk about "self-alienation"—estrangement from or failure to actualize one's "true self"—becomes intelligible.

The third basic element of the Marxian theory of alienation is the idea of man's alienation from his fellow men. The competitive social relationships of the market system make genuine community impossible by producing egoistic individuals who view others only as means toward satisfying their own desires—virtually insatiable desires for material wealth which are themselves artifacts of the system, not "natural" desires of all human beings regardless of what sort of society they live in. It is at this point that the argument from exploitation and the argument from alienation overlap: both charge that the market system fosters the harmful, merely instrumental utilization of human beings by other human beings.

Disalienation and Positive Freedom   It can be argued that the Marxian conception of alienation is at least closely related to the concept of *positive freedom* and that the latter concept provides important links between the three elements of the Marxian conception that were just outlined.[37] Very roughly, the distinction between negative and positive freedom is said to be as follows. Negative freedom consists merely in *freedom from interferences* by the actions of other human beings; positive freedom is the *freedom to pursue* effectively what one freely chooses to pursue. Most importantly, positive freedom requires that the individual have access to material resources needed for the successful pursuit of his chosen goals, while negative freedom (ordinarily) does not.

The distinction between positive and negative freedom, as presented, is far from unproblematic. Some have rejected it on the grounds that freedom is always freedom *from something, to do something*.[38] Others have argued that talk about positive freedom confuses freedom with opportunity or ability. Here I will make no attempt to resolve this complex issue. My aim, rather, is to trace the connections between the concept of positive freedom, or perhaps more accurately, a particular conception of autonomy, and the three elements of the Marxian theory of alienation.[39]

It is clear that even if one enjoys negative freedom—freedom from certain interferences by other persons—one can still suffer from alienation in the sense of loss of control over human creations that react harmfully against their creators. Or to put the point in a positive fashion, disalienation, in the first sense, requires more than negative liberty; it requires effective control over social institutions and relations. And if being dominated by one's own creations is a form of heteronomy, then full autonomy requires rational control over them and disalienation involves the enhancement of autonomy.

Further, according to Marx, effective, rational control over the natural and social environment must be *collective* control exercised by a genuine community of human beings. Marx, like some democratic theorists with whom he shares little else in common, tends to think of equal participation in collective control as a component of the fullest expression of individual autonomy or positive freedom. Consequently, disalienation in the sense of overcoming man's estrangement from his fellows, through equal participation in collective control, is also thought of as the achievement of positive freedom or autonomy.

Finally, Marxians also sometimes subsume the remaining element of the theory of alienation, the idea of self-actualization, under a concept of positive freedom or autonomy. Self-actualization requires more than merely negative freedom; it requires the freedom (or ability) to pursue effectively one's chosen goals and to develop one's talents as one sees fit. And according to this view, it will only be possible for all human beings (as opposed to a privileged minority) freely to pursue their own goals and to develop their talents if they live in a social system that is subject to a process of rational collective control, in which each can participate as an equal. Further, it is claimed that only such a system can provide the material abundance necessary for the all-around development of *all* individuals, while at the same time avoiding the stunting effects of the division of labor and the egoistic competition that are characteristic of the market system. In other words, alienation can be avoided only in a system which simultaneously satisfies three very ambitious conditions: (1) it must be *democratic* (that is, each must enjoy roughly equal control over productive resources); (2) it must be efficient enough to provide everyone with the material resources for self-actualization; and (3) it must avoid the narrow specialization and regimentation in the workplace that is said to be characteristic of capitalism.

It is vital to realize that alienation, so understood, is not even in principle restricted to social systems in which there is *private property* in the means of production, if by 'private property' we mean only one form of *minority control*—that is, control over productive resources by the few to the exclusion of control by the many. For the individual producer will lack control over his productive activity and over what he creates, and the majority will lack control over the social institutions and relations which they produce and perpetuate, regardless of whether exclusive, minority control over productive resources is exercised by individuals as individuals (as in the *private* property system of capitalism) or by individuals as members of a subgroup (as in the *collective* property system of state socialism). In either case the majority is excluded from control over productive resources, and this lack of control, according to Marx, is the root cause of alienation in all its manifestations. From this it follows that according to the Marxian theory of alienation itself, the abolition of private property is only necessary but not sufficient for the overcoming of alienation. Alienation will end only if all systems of exclusionary, minority control over productive resources (whether of the individual or the collective sort) are replaced by a system of nonexclusionary, that is, genuinely democratic control.

Marx, like many democratic theorists, including Rousseau, may have indulged in a dubious assumption: that a system which is democratic in the sense that no one has greater control over decisions than anyone else will be a system in which each enjoys a significant degree of control. But Rousseau's stirring rhetoric notwithstanding, it is the majority, not the individual, who is in control even in the most strict, direct, participatory democracy. It follows that if alienation is rooted in the individual's lack of control over his productive activity and its fruits, then even the most thoroughly democratic system for controlling production would not necessarily eliminate alienation. Similarly, abolishing private property in the means of production (or collective minority control over the means of production) and establishing democratic control does not eliminate the possibility of exploitation— exploitation of a minority by the majority, for example.

There are two quite distinct ways to understand the criticism that the private property market system produces alienation. As a radical criticism, it is the uncompromising Marxian view that alienation is an unacceptable condition for human beings and that the only way to get rid of the alienation we now suffer from in capitalism is to get rid of capitalism. In other words, as a genuinely radical argument, the argument from alienation calls for the total abolition of the private property market system. As a reformist or meliorist criticism, the argument from alienation is much more modest: it calls for efforts to reduce alienation, where possible, by modifying the private property market system in various ways, for example, by achieving a degree of "worker control" within firms that still operate in a largely capitalistic system.

The extent to which the reformist or meliorist approach to the problems of alienation in the private property market system is successful is a complex empirical issue that is clearly beyond the scope of the present work. Since my aim is to articulate the presuppositions of arguments for and against the market, I shall limit myself to two main points. First, the reformist approach simply assumes what the radical or Marxian version of the argument vigorously denies, namely, that a significant reduction of alienation can occur in a system in which control over productive resources is still to a large extent exercised by a minority, as it is in any market system in which private property continues to play a major role in social organization. Second, if the radical or Marxian version of the argument from alienation is to go beyond a purely destructive condemnation of the current system and offer a constructive proposal for ending alienation, it must first provide a genuine *theory* of the unalienated society (as opposed to a mere vision of it,), and it must then show that the implementation of that theory is practically possible. If, as I have argued, the Marxian is committed to the view that alienation can only be overcome by a system of highly efficient, genuinely democratic control, then this first step raises a number of difficulties which have already been examined in earlier sections of this work. In particular, the needed theory of social organization must show how the goals of efficiency and democracy (that is, at least some rough approximation of equal control) each can be realized without compromising the other. This, as we saw earlier, is an extremely difficult task, since the standard strategies for avoiding inefficiency in democratic procedures come at the price of abandoning the goal of equal participation.

Appreciating these major lacunae in the radical argument from alienation should not blind us to the seriousness of the charge that the market system produces alienation. Even if alienation can and does exist in nonmarket systems and even if an adequate theory of a nonalienating alternative system is lacking, it does not follow that the argument from alienation can simply be dismissed. In particular, it will not do simply to conclude that alienation in the market system is the price we must pay for efficiency, for to do so would be to assume that considerations of efficiency always take precedence over moral considerations. A less dogmatic approach would recognize that some forms of alienation are so serious that some reductions in efficiency are worth the price of ameliorating them. Once again, considerations which are incapable of showing that the market system ought to be scrapped may nevertheless provide plausible grounds for restrictions on the market.

The Market and Nonmarket Forms of Interaction

The Expansionist Tendency of the Market   The last type of argument to be considered is at the same time less concrete and more profound than any examined thus far. It begins with a straightforward empirical hypothesis, namely, that market relations tend to expand into areas of human life which previously had been outside the scope of the market. There is little doubt that this tendency has been at work at least in Western European cultures in the past several centuries, though generalized predictions as to whether the scope of market relations will continue to widen or has already begun to contract are much more controversial. 'Market relations' here refers not only to the physical activities of exchange, but also to the legal institutions, and even ways of thinking which are characteristic of the market. Indeed it is something of a commonplace among economic historians that one of the chief factors which accelerated the expansion of market relations was the emergence of the *idea of a market,* most notably in the works of writers such as Adam Ferguson and Adam Smith.

The Degradation of Valued Forms of Human Interaction   At this point in the argument a deeply felt but far from transparent normative premise is added to the empirical hypothesis: if left unchecked, the expansion of market relations will encroach (if it has not already done so) upon spheres of human interaction in which market relations do not belong, with the result that certain valuable human relationships will be degraded if not utterly extinguished.

The fear that the market drives out other forms of valuable interaction and attitudes is evident even in the classical exponents of the market. Adam Smith, for example, observed regretfully that the growth of commerce reduces the "martial spirit," by which he may have meant not militant or violent attitudes per se, but rather the patriotic spirit that moves men and women to risk their lives and fortunes for the sake of their country.[40] Hegel expressed a related concern when he urged that it would be a profound mistake to understand—and participate in—intimate personal relationships such as marriage and the family as if they were the sorts of self-interested, calculating juridicial relationships that are characteristic of interactions in the market.[41] According to Hegel, in a marriage or a family that is functioning as it should be—that is, in the mode which makes these intimate relationships distinctively valuable—individuals do not characteristically conceive of themselves as having independent and distinct interests and as employing the artifice of a contract to assign rights and duties in a calculated quid pro quo. Instead the members of a family or the partners in a marriage identify with each other's interests and relate to one another through spontaneous concern and sympathy.

Some modern writers, including David Gauthier in an article whose Hegelian roots he frankly acknowledges, attempt to extend this point beyond the sphere of intimate personal relationships, in a fashion that is consonant with our earlier interpretation of Smith's remark about the incompatibility of the commercial mentality and the martial spirit. Gauthier contends that the sustaining sentiments of intimate relationships and patriotism have this much in common: they are both practical attitudes which are antithetical to the calculating, self-interested, or individual utility-maximizing motivation of *homo economicus,* or market man.[42]

Yet another version of the normative thesis is offered by Richard Titmuss in his famous study, *The Gift Relationship.*[43] Titmuss contrasts the systems for collecting human blood for medical uses in Great Britain and in the United States. He argues that in Great Britain, where there is no developed market in which human blood is bought and sold, the giving of blood has a different, and indeed a higher significance than it does in a society in which blood has a monetary price like any other commodity. He cites statements by donors in Great Britain which show that they believe giving blood is especially important precisely because blood does not (in that society) have a market value. Titmuss concludes that this recognition of the special status of blood, an attitude which is incompatible with the existence of a developed market in blood, stimulates the springs of altruism. Peter Singer makes more explicit an additional conclusion: if we allow market relations to dominate most or all spheres of human activity, we may no longer be motivationally capable of certain forms of altruism.[44] Although there is much dispute over Titmuss's interpretation of the data and even more about the scope and validity of the generalization that the market drives out altruism, there is a great deal of plausibility to the more guarded claim that human life would be greatly impoverished if all interpersonal relationships were market relationships.

As the remarks of Smith, Hegel, Gauthier, and Titmuss show, the charge that the market threatens to degrade valuable forms of human interaction is much broader and deeper than the slogan, encountered much earlier in this chapter, that capitalism treats sex as a commodity. Nonetheless, perhaps the most graphic and familiar example of the alleged imperialist tendencies of the market is the assimilation of sexual relations to market transactions.

Some prominent contemporary economists have not been reluctant to extend the market model to the *explanation* of sexual behavior. Richard McKenzie and Gordon Tullock, for example, have hypothesized that the frequency of sexual intercourse for a couple can be viewed as the outcome of nonmonetary exchanges in which each partner strives to

> consume sex up to the point that the marginal benefits equal the marginal costs (or until $MU_s/P_s = MU_a/P_a = \ldots MU_n/P_n$, where *Mu* and *P* denote marginal utility and price, respectively, and where *s* represents sex and *a* and *n*, other goods). If the price of sex rises relative to other goods, the consumer will rationally choose to consume more of other goods and less sex. (Ice cream, as well as many other goods, can substitute for sex if the relative prices require it.)[45]

McKenzie and Tullock, like others who attempt to explain various forms of intimate behavior using the market model, are quick to note that they are concerned only with explaining how people do behave, not with prescribing how they ought to. They do not even raise the question of whether the presence of market attitudes and behavior in this sphere of personal interaction is degrading or in any way undesirable. Nor do they consider whether there is a relationship between the increasing acceptance of the market model as the appropriate form of explanation for a certain sphere of human activity and the growing tendency of that sphere of activity to fit the market model. Yet it was noted earlier that it is something of a platitude that one factor which accelerates the expansion of market relations is the recognition that there is a market and that we are exchangers in it. In other words, to the extent that we come to view our interactions as market transactions they may actually come more closely to approximate the model by which we seek to explain them.

A being who reflects upon his own activity, seeking to understand it, may thereby alter his conception of himself. But if we change our conception of ourselves profoundly, we may change ourselves. The economist's self-congratulatory claim that his market analysis of human relationships is value-neutral would then be a sad self-deception.

4

Market Socialism—Separating the Market from Private Property in the Means of Production

Two Types of Market Socialism

Thus far the focus has been on the market with private property in the means of production, that is, market capitalism, or simply capitalism. Now we shall examine systems which utilize the market as a basic institution for coordinating social activity in the absence of private ownership of the means of production: market socialism.

Two distinct types of system are widely discussed in the literature under this label. The first, which was articulated in the 1930s, and achieved its most influential formulation by the economists Oskar Lange and Fred M. Taylor, may be called consumer and labor market socialism, to indicate that the scope of the market is restricted to a market for consumer goods and for labor, with no market for production goods (means of production).[1] For convenience we shall refer to this first type of market socialism simply as the Taylor-Lange model. The second variety of market socialism extends the scope of the market to include not only labor and consumer goods but also a market for production goods. This second type also includes another element which is not part of the Taylor-Lange model: "democratic" worker control over the means of production at the level of the individual firm or enterprise. In the real world system that most clearly approximates this second type, the Yugoslav economy since the early 1950s, worker control and markets for labor, consumer goods, and production goods are found together. Further, in the theoretical literature these two distinct features are also combined. So while worker control might be united with the more restricted role for markets of the Taylor-Lange model and although there is no conceptual or practical barrier to constructing a model which utilizes markets for production goods as well as for labor and consumer goods but which does not include worker control, we shall examine the actual combinations of these different elements that are historically and theoretically prominent. For this reason the second type may be referred to either as 'consumer-labor-production market socialism' or simply 'the worker control model.'[2] Both models warrant the title 'socialism' because each features public, rather than private ownership of the means of production.

The Taylor-Lange model includes the following elements:

1. There is a market for labor (with freedom in the choice of occupations).

2. There is a market for consumer goods (in which individuals use their incomes to purchase what they desire).

3. The means of production are (for the most part) publicly owned, that is, controlled ultimately by the central government.

4. There is no market for production goods. The government, functioning through a Central Planning Board, formulates and executes a plan that specifies how productive resources (production goods) are allocated. This plan also includes an investment plan which determines the rate, types, and amount of investment.

5. In order to allocate resources efficiently, the Central Planning Board must determine the relative values of various production goods. In the absence of a market for such goods, and hence in the absence of market prices for them, the Central Planning Board at first arbitrarily assigns prices to production goods and then adjusts and readjusts these prices using a trial and error method of successive approximation. It raises the price of a production good if the consumer market reveals a shortage of the consumer goods produced from the production good in question; it lowers the price if the consumer market reveals an oversupply.

6. Managers of firms (at all levels) are to follow two rules: (a) combine productive resources so as to minimize average cost of production, and (b) produce at a scale of output at which the marginal cost of the product equals the price of the product.

In contrast, the worker control variety of market socialism allows all prices, including prices of production goods, to be determined by market processes. The function of the central government is correspondingly less ambitious.

1. The central government develops an investment plan, raising investment funds from taxing the profits of firms, but it does not set prices for goods. The central government also intervenes when necessary to minimize unemployment.
2. Worker-managed firms compete for the consumer market and for investment funds which the central government lends to them at an interest rate which it determines.
3. The workers in a firm determine not only what to produce and how to produce it, but also how to divide among themselves the profits the enterprise earns on the market.
4. Worker management is democratic in that each worker has a vote in determining the basic structure of management, but the workers in a given firm may democratically decide to delegate authority for management decisions, even bringing in professional managers if they wish.

It is important to emphasize that these four elements define the theoretical model of worker management socialism to be examined in what follows. They are not intended as accurate characterizations of the Yugoslav economy. For example, central investment planning in that country is now greatly reduced if not virtually defunct.

Market Socialism and the Socialist Tradition: The Great Concession   Before proceeding to an examination of the two models, it is necessary to reflect upon the significance of market socialism for the socialist tradition. The emergence of the theory and practice of market socialism is a profound concession on the part of the socialist tradition, and a significant departure from some of the most basic views of Marx, the founder of modern socialism. Marx never took seriously the possibility of a market system without private property in the means of production in a modern, industrialized society. Moreover, it would be false to say that Marx's failure to consider a separation of the market from private property was a mere oversight, implying that a distinction between the market and capitalism could be made without significantly revising his critique of capitalism.[3]

There are at least two key elements of Marx's critique of capitalism which focus directly upon the nature of the market, and are not tied in any direct way to private property in the means of production. First, there is the charge that, as a system that lacks an overall rational plan for coordinating social activity, the market is "anarchy in production," and that this anarchy will inevitably and repeatedly result in massive waste and severe social and economic instability. A more specific application of this general point is Marx's contention that a system which separates production from use, one in which the goal of producing something (that is, to maximize profit) is only indirectly connected with the goal of consuming what is produced (that is, to enhance the well-being of the consumer), must be less efficient than a system in which production and consumption are not thusly "separated." Second, and of equal importance for Marx, is the charge that any system, including the market, that relies upon motivation which is competitive, rather than directly cooperative, and which not only legitimizes, but even encourages conflicts of interests, cannot be the most efficient or the most humane form of social coordination. Whether Marx thought competitive motivation was in some sense intrinsically wrong or whether he only regarded it is as bad by virtue of its effects may not be clear, but there can be little doubt that he thought any society which found it necessary to rely upon the competition of limited, conflicting interests as the basic motivational force for social coordination was a defective, underdeveloped society.[4] While some Marxian socialists may still nurture the hope that market socialism is only a temporary stage in the transition from capitalism to a "higher," nonmarket socialism (or communism), there is at present no adequate theory of the transition from market to nonmarket socialism, nor, as we shall see, is there a practically applicable theory of the efficient operation of nonmarket socialism, that is, the centrally planned economy.

It would be a mistake to conclude that market socialism represents only a departure from two key tenets of *Marxian socialism*. The concession to the market that this type of socialism makes is an abandonment of two rationalist ideals which Marx espoused but which have played a much larger role in modern thought. One is the Postmedieval ideal of man as the rational planner and controller of his natural and social environment. This is the vision of man as active engineer of nature and society, the being whose science not only reveals a perfectly intelligible universe, but also gives him the practical knowledge to shape that universe to his own ends. The second rationalist ideal goes beyond the imputation of virtually limitless knowledge, whether theoretical or practical. It is the vision of man as a being who is capable of altruistic, directly cooperative motivation, a being who does not oppose his own interests, or those of his close associates, to the good of the larger society. In some instances this ideal of communitarian motivation represents a longing for the close bonds of (a highly idealized) preindustrial society. But so far as it is espoused consistently with the first ideal, it expresses the conviction that the current lack of communitarian motivation is a result of ignorance and defective social conditions, both of which can be remedied by man, the rational planner of the natural and social environment.

Market socialism, if it does not signal an abandonment of both of these ideals, at least represents a retreat from the belief that they can be fully realized in the foreseeable future. On the one hand, market socialism (of both types) abandons the attempt to subject the entire economy to deliberate, rational control through planning. On the other, at least in the worker control version, it sharply limits communitarian motivation for economic activity to the level of the individual firm and uses competition among firms as the engine of efficiency. The movement from planned, nonmarket socialism to market socialism, then, represents a more pessimistic (or realistic) reassessment of two ideals which, though fundamental in the development of socialism, are not peculiar to it but are constitutive features of modern rationalist thought.[5]

The popularity of market socialism is obviously an impressive testimony to the power of the market as a basic institution for social coordination. However, the market socialists' appreciation of the market did not come easily. It can be traced to widespread dissatisfaction with both the theory and the practice of the other archetypal socialist model: planned socialism—the public ownership system which abolishes markets and attempts to solve all basic problems of allocation, production, and distribution through rational planning decisions, whether democratic or elitist.

The experience of the Soviet Union, especially during the period of war communism when rejection of the market was most complete, is taken by many to be sufficient evidence of the unacceptability of a thoroughly planned socialism in practice. It is often pointed out that even though comprehensive planning "works" in the present-day Soviet Union (to the extent that there is considerable economic growth, not simply an absence of massive economic breakdown), the cost to individual liberty is unacceptable. Further, there is considerable dispute as to how well the Soviet economy would function if the ideal of planning were more closely approximated than it in fact is. In particular, there is evidence that black (that is, illegal) markets play a significant role in the Soviet economy, providing a safety valve for economic and political dissatisfaction arising from the failures of planning.

However, quite independently of how one weighs the successes and failures of the Soviet experience with planned socialism, there is a theoretical reason for the popularity of market socialism and the disenchantment with planned socialism. To understand it we must examine the two types of market socialism just discussed in the light of the "Socialist Calculation Debate"—a controversy which has smoldered for fifty years, periodically erupting in conflagrations that have often produced more heat than light.

The Socialist Calculation Debate

The beginning of the debate is usually considered to be an article in which the Austrian economist Ludwig Von Mises argues that "rational economic activity is impossible in a socialist commonwealth . . . ."[6] Mises noted that rational economic activity requires the most efficient allocation of productive resources, and that this in turn requires a knowledge of *prices* for production goods, that is, quantitative values which can be compared in calculations. He then concluded that since these prices are determined by the interaction of buyers and sellers in the market, a socialist system, lacking a market for production-goods, would provide no way of determining, for purposes of efficient allocation, the relative values of various productive resources.

Before Mises's argument can be evaluated it must be interpreted. First, what does Mises include under the heading of "socialist commonwealth"? At the time he was writing (1920) the idea of market socialism, of either the Lange-Taylor or worker management types, had not yet been articulated. 'Socialism,' during this period in which the Marxian tradition was dominant, meant centrally planned socialism: public ownership of the means of production without markets. Second, when Mises says that rational allocation of production resources, and hence rational economic activity, is "impossible" in socialism, does he mean "impossible in principle" or "unachievable in practice"?

The structure of Mises's argument may require only that 'socialism' refers to a system of public ownership of the means of production in which there is *no market for production goods*, leaving open the possibility that, as in the Taylor-Lange model, there are markets for labor and consumer goods. However, nothing Mises says suggests that he defined 'socialism' so as to cover any type of market socialism, and the historical context in which he writes indicates that his argument was directed against planned socialism.

If Mises thought that rational allocation decisions are in principle (theoretically) impossible in planned socialism, that is, in the absence of markets, he was wrong. The consensus of informed opinion among economists is now that the mathematics of these calculations were available and were for the most part already well understood by the economists Barone and Pareto twenty years before Mises's article appeared.[7]

However, the mathematics, which require the solving of *millions* of simultaneous equations, whose variables are constantly changing over time, are so enormously complex that this method of determining relative values of productive resources is now generally regarded as impractical. In his contribution to the debate, Friederich Hayek argued, accordingly, that the more plausible interpretation of Mises's argument is *epistemological*, rather than logical. Even if the relevant equations could in principle be solved, the amount of information that would have to be fed into the equations could not be successfully absorbed by any one mind or any group of planners.[8]

Hayek's epistemological argument does not rest simply upon the staggering *amount* of information required. He also stresses that the information needed to determine the relative values of productive resources is so highly *particular* and *concrete* that it could not be adequately represented in statistical information of the sort which the central planners would of necessity rely upon. The information relevant to rational allocation decisions, Hayek notes, concerns the condition and disposition of particular machines and skilled workers, knowledge about available production space in various locales, and so forth. In addition, Hayek emphasizes that the relevant information is constantly shifting, as new technologies become available, as old raw materials deplete and new ones are discovered, and as consumers' preferences change. The wonder of the market, Hayek observes, is that it is able to utilize vast amounts of very concrete, particularized information, and to adjust economic activity automatically as this information changes.

While Hayek's epistemological argument may be a decisive objection to planned, nonmarket socialism, its efficacy against market socialism is subject to dispute. It is true that Hayek himself attempted to extend his critique to the Taylor-Lange model.[9] However, although Hayek and his supporters have somehow failed to notice it, the Taylor-Lange model provides a powerful reply to the charge that the information required by the central government would be more concrete and particular than the information that would be available to it.[10] According to the Taylor-Lange model, the Central Planning Board need not ferret out such concrete, particular bits of information. Instead, it looks at the *results* of many individual interactions in which concrete, particular information is utilized by individual consumers and producers. The Central Planning Board needs only to be able to recognize shortages and surpluses of consumer goods when they occur.

Further, as Lange points out, the trial and error method of successive approximations is based upon the fundamental principle of price theory for the perfectly competitive market. That principle states that if producers price their goods too high, demand will drop, producers will notice this decrease in demand (as they see their inventories expanding), and will lower their prices. Similarly, if producers set prices too low, demand will increase, and if producers notice that their production is not keeping pace with demand, they will raise prices. In other words, the type of information required by the Central Planning Board on the Taylor-Lange model is no more concrete or particular than the information about demand that must be known by the individual producer in the free market—indeed it is the same information. Just as information of the existence of shortages and surpluses is usd by producers in the free market to adjust prices set initially at some point by producers, so the same information is used by the Central Planning Board in the Taylor-Lange model to adjust prices after they are initially set by the board. Further, as Lange also emphasizes, the board need not even set initial prices arbitrarily. It can set them at recent historical levels or copy them from a currently existing free market economy.

It is true, of course, that the Central Planning Board would have to gather and assimilate a larger *amount* of information than any individual producer in the free market would require, but this does not seem by itself to be an insurmountable problem, given anticipated advances in computerized technology for data processing. If Hayek's argument is to provide a telling objection to the Taylor-Lange model, then, it must be formulated as the criticism that the trial and error price adjustments would have to be so frequent and the cost of constantly gathering and evaluating data about shortages and surpluses would be so high, that even if the method were workable, it would be significantly less efficient than a capitalist market system.

This version of the argument is difficult to assess, for two reasons. First, since there seems to be no way to demonstrate theoretically that the trial and error method would suffer from serious inefficiencies, empirical studies of the performance of such a system over time are needed. They are not available, however, because existing socialist systems more closely resemble the planned socialist model or the worker management model than the Taylor-Lange model. Second, there are the difficulties, noted earlier, of any attempt to make reliable and fairly precise comparisons of the efficiency of different types of systems.

If Hayek's epistemological argument is less than decisive against the Taylor-Lange model, it appears to be even weaker when applied to the worker management variety of market socialism. Since it includes a market for production goods among competing firms and since prices for production goods as well as consumer goods arise through the market process, the worker management model seems to avoid the epistemological difficulties not only of planned socialism but also any remaining problems that might arise in the Taylor-Lange model due to the lack of a genuine market for production goods.

Matters are not quite so simple, however. Both the Taylor-Lange model and worker management include at least one important planning function for the central government: investment planning. If the information requirements and the information processing costs for overall investment planning are sufficiently high, then the epistemological objection can be raised at the level of investment planning. Again, the most plausible version of the argument would maintain, not that such planning is in theory impossible, nor even that it is in practice unworkable, but rather that it is less efficient than a system in which investment is left mainly to market forces.

Hayek, in an explicit critique of Lange, raises yet another version of the epistemological objection.[11] He predicts that in order to monitor the performance of managers, the central government would have to engage in frequent and detailed audits of each firm's accounting records. In particular, it would be necessary, though extremely costly and perhaps rather ineffective, to make sure that managers are faithfully observing the rule that they are to minimize average costs of production.

This objection is stated by Hayek as an epistemological criticism, but it may be more illuminating to view it as only one instance of a very general problem for the Taylor-Lange model, a problem which is more properly *motivational* than epistemological. The need for monitoring managers arises because the Taylor-Lange model fails to provide a theory of incentives for managers. In the capitalist market, the system provides its own incentive, the profit motive, for ensuring that production costs are kept down. The market "monitors" managerial performance through competition and simple self-interest drives the competition.

In the Taylor-Lange model there is no competition among firms. Whether or not managers will be sufficiently motivated to follow the rules for efficient production will depend upon whether an adequate system of rewards (and/or punishments) can be developed which is not itself so costly as to impair efficiency. In the absence of effective incentives, a monitoring system as detailed and costly as the one Hayek envisions could become a necessity.

In addition, the needed incentive system must be capable of motivating managers without doing so in such a way as to undercut what proponents of the Taylor-Lange model take to be one of its greatest attractions: the more equal distribution of income it would allow. If the chief motivation for good managerial performance in the system turns out to be higher wages, then the socialist goal of a more nearly equal distribution of income will be that much farther from attainment.

In sum, the Taylor-Lange model shows an appreciation for one important feature of the market: the relationship of reciprocal adjustment between prices, on the one hand, and supply and demand, on the other, as expressed in the fundamental principle of price theory. But this model seems blind to a second crucial feature of the market— its motivational power, the way in which the market harnesses self-interest to achieve mutual benefit.

The worker control variety of market socialism escapes at least one objection to which the Taylor-Lange model is vulnerable. Worker control does not require the trial and error method's frequent and potentially costly surveys of shortages and surpluses, because it allows prices for production goods to be set by the market. However, as with the Taylor-Lange model, the centralized planning of overall investment requires complex and frequently revised data and calculations. Moreover, the costs of such an arrangement are not likely to be purely financial. The power to control overall investment, like any concentrated power, is likely to be abused, especially in a system in which there is public ownership of the means of production.

Here also, a motivational component must be supplied to the market socialist model if the objection is to be satisfactorily met. In this case, what is required is a theory of bureaucratic incentives. In both types of market socialism the need for such a theory is especially acute since by hypothesis investment decisions are not directly linked, as they are in a capitalist market system, to the preferences of consumers expressed in the market.

Of course, the proponent of market socialism may reply that the central government's investment decisions will be tied to consumer preferences by suitable democratic political processes. But at this point the theoretical task becomes larger, not smaller. The market socialist must explain not only how planners will be motivated to follow government policies on investment but also how democratic processes will ensure that government policy accurately reflects consumer preferences.

The worker control model has been subjected to sharp criticism concerning the motivation not only of managers but also of workers in subordinate positions. Benjamin Ward has argued that since profits will be shared in the worker-managed firm, workers will strive to maximize income per worker, that is, average income, rather than total income.[12] He then concludes that worker-conrolled firms will not have a sufficient incentive to expand production, where this means hiring new workers, in response to price increases for the firm's product. Expanding production, where this includes hiring more workers, would simply mean that total income would have to be divided among more individuals.[13]

The problem Ward raises is really only one instance of a much more general difficulty for worker management. Granted that income is to be shared in some rather egalitarian way, the connection between individual effort and individual reward becomes attenuated. Under such conditions, the familiar free-rider and assurance problems may arise. Especially in a large firm, the individual may be tempted to act on the following reasoning. "My compensation will be determined by how hard and how well the firm as a whole, or the majority of its employees work. Granted that my contribution is small, whether or not I expend maximal effort will not noticeably affect overall success."

It is important to note, of course, that free-riding on the efforts of others is far from uncommon in capitalist enterprises, especially large ones. The point, however, is that the capitalist manager or firm owner has an obvious weapon to combat the problem, namely, wage differentials according to estimated individual marginal productivity, and also has a strong incentive, the desire to maximize profits, to use this weapon.

Proponents of market socialism may quickly reply that the workers can vote for differential pay proportionate to productivity if they wish. This remedy, however, is one which the market socialist must use sparingly. Large pay differentials, even if they would be voted by the majority, threaten to erode one major source of the alleged superiority of worker management: greater equality in the distribution of income.

Similarly, genuinely democratic management may be an unstable option in market socialism. If, for example, the time costs of democratic decision-making in the firm are a significant source of inefficiency, competition among firms will erode democratic management. For even if the workers in each firm were willing to forgo the greater efficiency of nondemocratic management if they could be assured that other firms would do so as well, each group of workers will have an incentive, namely, the desire to maintain a competitive position, to violate purely voluntary agreements to preserve democracy. But if such agreements are enforced, then democracy will be sustained at the price of inefficiency.

Market socialists of both types maintain that their systems are superior to private property market systems on two other grounds: they are better able to cope with externalities and with unemployment. Let us consider each of these two points in turn.

It should be clear that the same competitive forces that produce externalities (such as pollution) in private property market systems will also produce externalities in worker management market socialism. In both cases, competition encourages producers and consumers to disregard social costs that are not reflected in market prices. Whether one system does a better job of coping with externalities will in general depend, then, upon how successful government intervention in the market is.

Market socialists argue that government is likely to be more successful in handling externalities where there is public rather than private ownership of the means of production. This, however, is not obvious, either empirically or in theory. Some countries in which public ownership of the means of production is most nearly complete, such as the USSR, have rather abominable records on the control of externalities such as pollution. Moreover, whether or not a market system with public ownership will in principle do a better job with externalities cannot even be deduced from the theory of market socialism in the absence of an account of bureaucratic motivation.

Finally, even if a public ownership system would enjoy the advantage of not having to overcome the resistance of politically powerful private interests in dealing with externalities, it would also lack one strategy available to a capitalist market system. In a market system in which there is private ownership of the means of production, externalities can in some cases be "internalized," as we saw in chapter 2, by assigning private property rights where none previously existed. It is far from apparent, then, that market socialism is superior to a regulated private property system on the score of externalities. And even if it could be conclusively shown that market socialism was superior in its ability to deal with these problems, this would not be sufficient to establish its overall preferability if the source of its greater capability for dealing with externalities, public ownership of the means of production, creates a dangerous concentration of power.

Nor is there anything in either type of market socialism to guarantee that unemployment will not be a problem. However, both versions do include a mechanism, government control of investment, for minimizing unemployment. The idea is that by setting an appropriate investment policy and an appropriate income support policy to implement wages at the lower end of the scale, the government can, in Keynesian fashion, ensure that sufficient consumer demand is maintained to sustain growth.

If the main lines of the Keynesian analysis of unemployment are accepted, it is apparent that the two types of market socialism *in principle* will do a better job of coping with unemployment than a laissez-faire, that is, virtually unregulated, capitalist market system. But then again no laissez-faire system exists (nor ever did). It is far less clear that either variety of market socialism in practice would be significantly better at reducing unemployment than an interventionist private property or "mixed capitalist" system. Indeed the rather good unemployment records of Japan and the Scandinavian countries (and the very poor unemployment record of Yugoslavia) in recent years add weight to this conclusion.

We have already seen that in worker control the tendency to maximize average rather than total revenues in the firm creates its own distinctive unemployment problem since firms will not respond to increased prices by hiring more workers, where returns to scale are constant. David Schweikart, a forceful defender of worker control, has argued that worker "solidarity" would ease the problem of unemployment and that the workers' sense of "social responsibility" would counteract the tendency toward underexpansion.[14]

The problem with this reply is not simply that the sense of solidarity which it invokes may result in inefficiency by overutilization of labor power under conditions of shrinking demand. A more basic difficulty is that Schweikart's reply assumes a bifurcation in the workers' motivation which, unless properly explained, may seem to border on the schizophrenic. Like other proponents of worker control market socialism, Schweikart assumes competitive, nonaltruistic motivation when he is attempting to show that market socialism could match if not exceed the efficiency of market capitalism. Yet when confronted with an objection that market socialism has its own sources of inefficiency, he assumes a diametrically opposed sort of motivation. My point is not that Schweikert is literally inconsistent or that the two quite different sorts of motivation he ascribes to workers are psychologically incompatible. Instead I only wish to emphasize that here as elsewhere a successful defense of market socialism depends upon the development of a more adequate account of motivation.

There is one final source of inefficiency in market socialist systems which should not be overlooked, but whose magnitude, once again, may be difficult to ascertain. Both types of market socialist systems include a significant departure from the conditions for perfect competition insofar as government ownership of the means of production and government control of investment place restrictions on free entry to and exit from the market.

Conclusions

This brief survey of the complex and growing debate on market socialism is not intended to be comprehensive.[15] Its goals are much more limited. The first and most important of these is to make clear to what extent arguments for and against the market are directed toward the market itself and to what extent they apply only to the market with private property in the means of production. Second, I hope to have gone deeply enough into the matter to support, though not to demonstrate, one important conclusion which can serve as a starting point for further research. That conclusion is that even if planned socialism can be rejected as highly inefficient as well as inimical to individual liberty, market socialism cannot be dismissed as clearly unworkable or as obviously inferior—*on grounds of efficiency*—to politically feasible, nonideal, private property market systems. Although market socialist theory will remain seriously incomplete until appropriate theories of bureaucratic, managerial, and worker motivation are developed, market socialism is clearly an alternative to private ownership which must be taken seriously, even if we restrict our view to considerations of efficiency alone.

Given that a conclusive case one way or the other strictly on grounds of efficiency seems unlikely at present, ethical comparisons between private and public ownership market systems become all the more crucial. If, for example, genuinely democratic managment of firms is attainable—and if it results in a significant reduction of alienation in the work place as its advocates predict—this form of market socialism might prove superior on balance, even if it were somewhat less efficient than the private property market system. The comprehensive ethical assessment of market socialism, however, requires the articulation of a developed ethical theory of market socialism, as well as its integration with the economic theory of market socialism. Quite disparate ethical theories of market socialism are not difficult to imagine. On the one hand, it could be argued that market socialism does a better job of realizing the same basic liberal democratic values which defenders of the restrained capitalism of the welfare state purport to espouse. On the other hand, market socialism might be viewed as resting on an ideal of community and fulfillment through collective productive activity—values which some would argue are alien to liberal thought. At present the ethical theory of market socialism is considerably more rudimentary than its economic theory, but this situation shows signs of changing.[16]

Notes

Chapter 1

1. For a somewhat different, but overlapping explanation of different economic concepts of efficiency or different elements of the economic concept of efficiency, especially in relation to the use of the term 'efficiency' in the economic analysis of law, see Jules Coleman's article "Efficiency, Exchange and Auction: Philosophic Aspects of the Economic Approach to Law."

Some economists prefer the Kaldor (or Marshall) Efficiency Criterion over the Pareto principles. A social state is Kaldor Efficient if and only if there is no way of redistributing goods so that the total benefit to the gainers, measured by the sum of the numbers of dollars each would be willing to pay for the benefit, is larger than the total loss to the losers, similarly measured. There are several reasons why I shall concentrate on Pareto rather than Kaldor (or Marshall) Efficiency. First, I am concerned to provide a critical analysis of the dominant way of thinking about efficiency, and there can be little doubt that the Pareto approach is the most widely used notion of efficiency. In addition, there are sound theoretical reasons for preferring the Pareto principles. The Pareto principles only presuppose that different individuals' utilities can be compared in the weakest possible sense, namely, that when we say that a certain change would make A *better off* without making B *worse off*, we are in some sense talking about the same thing, that is, well-being. Kaldor (or Marshall) Efficiency presupposes interpersonal utility comparisons of a much stronger and highly controversial sort, since it assumes that cardinal interpersonal comparisons can be made (measured by willingness to pay). Finally, the use of the Kaldor (or Marshall) Efficiency Criterion leads to inconsistent preferences among social states: as Scitovsky has demonstrated, a state can be Kaldor Efficient to itself. For a more detailed discussion of Kaldor Efficiency, including the problem presented by The Scitovsky Paradox, see J. Coleman, "Efficiency, Utility, and Wealth Maximization."

2. See, for example, L. Robbins, *An Essay on the Nature and Significance of Economic Science*, p. 140. For two more critical treatments of the problem of interpersonal utility comparisons, see D. W. Brock, "Recent Work in Utilitarianism," pp. 245–49; and R. E. Sartorius, *Individual Conduct and Social Norms*, pp. 28–31.

3. All of the following works criticize the view that pleasure is a feeling or sensation. J. L. Cowan, *Pleasure and Pain* (New York, 1968); D. L. Perry, *The Concept of Pleasure* (London, 1968); J.C.B. Gosling, *Pleasure and Desire* (Oxford, 1969); G. Ryle, *Dilemmas* (Cambridge, Eng., 1954).

4. J. M. Buchanan makes this point in "Order Defined in the Process of Its Emergence," p. 5. Coleman distinguishes between (1) the claim that Pareto Optimality or Pareto Superiority judgments warrant claims about the maximization of utility, and (2) the claim that the justification for pursuing Pareto Superior states is that doing so maximizes utility. Coleman also notes that a move to a Pareto Optimal state does not necessarily increase utility (since the antecedent state may have been Pareto Optimal).

He then points out that the pursuit of Pareto improvements may be justified on nonutilitarian grounds ("Efficiency, Utility, and Wealth Maximization," pp. 509–51).

5. Jules Coleman makes the point that preference is not equivalent to consent and notes that some leading work in the economic approach to law erroneously takes these notions as equivalent. See his "Economics and the Law: A Critical Review of the Foundations of the Economic Approach to Law," pp. 671–77.

6. Russell Hardin, "Difficulties in the Notion of Economic Rationality," *Social Science Information*, forthcoming.

Chapter 2

1. Any standard microeconomic textbook provides an explanation of why the general equilibrium of production and exchange in the ideal market is Pareto Optimal. The usual, and perhaps the most illuminating method of explanation employs a graphic representation which combines the Edgeworth Box and indifference curves. For two of the clearest and most detailed explanations of this type, see C. E. Ferguson and J. P. Gould, *Microeconomic Theory*, pp. 440–50; and A. Feldman, *Welfare Economics and Social Choice Theory*, pp. 27–37. R. H. Coase has shown that assumption (a) (no transaction costs) can substitute for assumption (b) (perfect competition and absence of externalities and public goods) because where transaction costs are zero, inefficiencies due to imperfect competition and externalities and public goods can be eliminated by bargains. See Coase, "The Problem of Social Cost."

2. F. A. Hayek, *The Constitution of Liberty*, pp. 54–70; Hayek, *Individualism and the Economic Order*, pp. 119–208.

3. J. Gray, "F. A. Hayek and the Rebirth of Classical Liberalism," p. 32.

4. B. Mandeville, *Fable of the Bees: Or Private Vices, Public Benefits;* and A. Smith, *The Wealth of Nations*, p. 14.

5. See, for example, G. J. Stigler, "The Theory of Economic Regulation."

6. W. Niskanen, *Bureaucracy and Representative Government;* Niskanen, "Bureaucrats and Politicians," pp. 617–53. See also D. Mueller, *Public Choice*, pp. 148–74. For a view of the regulation process that emphasizes the role of beliefs about fairness, see E. E. Zajac, *Fairness or Efficiency: An Introduction to Public Utility Pricing*.

7. For three of the most influential treatments of the problem of providing public goods, see J. M. Buchanan, *The Demand and Supply of Public Goods;* G. Hardin, "The Tragedy of the Commons," *Science* (December 13, 1968); and M. Olson, *The Logic of Collective Action*.

8. A clear presentation of economic analyses of principles of compensation is found in J. G. Murphy and J.L. Coleman, *The Philosophy of Law: An Introduction to Jurisprudence,* chapter 5. See also M. Kuperberg and C. Beitz, eds., *Law, Economics, and Philosophy: A Critical Introduction with Application to the Law of Torts*.

9. H. Demsetz, "Toward a Theory of Property Rights," pp. 347–59.

10. A. E. Buchanan, *Marx and Justice: The Radical Critique of Liberalism*, pp. 21–35. The author develops an account of the role of the concept of distorted desires in Marx's historical materialist theory of consciousness and in his evaluation of capitalism.

11. G. A. Cohen, "Labor, Leisure, and a Distinctive Contradiction of Advanced Capitalism," pp. 107–36.

12. "An Introduction to Markets and Morals," in G. Dworkin, G. Bermant, and P.G. Brown, eds., *Markets and Morals*, p. 8.

13. Cohen, "Distinctive Contradiction of Advanced Capitalism," in ibid., pp. 126–27.

14. For a more detailed presentation of the view that some of Marx's most serious criticisms of capitalism presuppose a theory of democratic social organizaiton which he lacks, see A. E. Buchanan, *Marx and Justice*, pp. 169–75; Buchanan, "Marx on Democracy and the Obsolescence of Rights," pp. 130–35. See also A.E. Buchanan, "The Fetishism of Democracy: A Reply to Professor Gould," pp. 729–31.

15. J. Locke, *Second Treatise of Civil Government*, chap. 5; and A. Smith, *The Wealth of Nations*, p. viii. For two excellent though somewhat technical essays on the problem

of intersystemic efficiency comparisons, see D. Conn, "The Evaluation of Centrally Planned Economic Systems: Methodological Precepts," pp. 15–46; and Conn, "Toward a Theory of Optimal Economic Systems," pp. 325–50.

16. J. Perry, "Personal Identity, Memory, and the Problem of Circularity," in *Personal Identity*, pp. 135–55; and Perry, "The Importance of Being Identical," in A. O. Rorty, ed., *Identities of Persons*, pp. 67–90.

17. This proposal was suggested to me by Jody Kraus.

18. David Friedman advances this argument in "Health on the Market," a paper presented at a conference on health care and the market, directed by B. Brody and sponsored by The Liberty Fund, Incorporated. In *Marx and Justice*, chap. 7, I used this same argument to criticize Marxists who assume that communism would be at least as efficient as capitalism, but who lack a theory of the economics of communism capable of supporting such a prediction.

Chapter 3

1. R. Hofstadter, *Social Darwinism in American Thought, 1860–1915.*

2. For a lucid examination of the concept of desert, see J. Feinberg, "Justice and Personal Desert," pp. 55–87.

3. D. W. Brock, "Recent Work in Utilitarianism," pp. 245–49, provides a valuable critical survey of utilitarian views.

4. This point is made and illustrated using the graph in Figure 3.1 by A. Lerner, *The Economics of Control*, pp. 28–31.

5. The position that utilitarianism would exclude some disabled individuals from a guaranteed "decent minimum" of goods and services is presented by A. K. Sen, *On Economic Inequality*, pp. 16ff. On pp. 316–19 of *A Theory of the Good and the Right*, R. B. Brandt defends the opposite position, attacking Sen.

6. A. E. Buchanan, "The Right to a Decent Minimum of Health Care."

7. Jules Coleman makes this point in "Efficiency, Exchange and Auction," pp. 221–49.

8. J. Rawls, *A Theory of Justice*, pp. 504–12.

9. T. Hobbes, *Leviathan*, parts I and II, chap. 12–21.

10. J. Locke, *Second Treatise of Civil Government*, chap. 1.

11. R. Nozick, *Anarchy, State, and Utopia*, pp. ix–x.

12. Ibid., pp. 178–82.

13. T. Nagel, "Libertarianism Without Foundations."

14. Nozick, *Anarchy, State, and Utopia*, pp. 160–64.

15. F. A. Hayek, *The Constitution of Liberty*, pp. 223–58.

16. G. A. Cohen, "Robert Nozick and Wilt Chamberlain: How Patterns Preserve Liberty," pp. 246–62.

17. Rawls, *A Theory of Justice*, pp. 136–41, 251–57.

18. A.E. Buchanan, "The Right to a Decent Minimum of Health Care," and "What's So Special About Rights?" For others who advance similar arguments for enforced beneficence, see S. Gorovitz, "Bigotry, Loyalty, and Malnutrition," in P. Brown and H. Shue, *Food Policy* (New York, 1977), pp. 140–41; H. Shue, *Basic Rights* (Princeton, N.J., 1980), chap. 6; and C. Beitz, *Political Theory and International Relations*, pt. 3 (Princeton, N.J., 1979).

19. This strategy was suggested to me by Jan Narveson.

20. Joel Feinberg suggests this conclusion in "The Moral and Legal Responsibility of the Bad Samaritan."

21. See, for example, R. B. McKenzie and G. Tullock, "Equal Pay for Equal Work," in *The New World of Economics.*

22. See, for example, M. Friedman, *Capitalism and Freedom*, Introduction and chap. 1.

23. For a clear analysis of moral arguments for private property, see L. Becker, *Property Rights: Philosophical Foundations.*

24. A provocative presentation of some relevant statistics is found in R. Quinney, *Class, State, and Crime,* pp. 136–39.

25. N. Daniels, "Equal Liberty and Unequal Worth of Liberty," in *Reading Rawls,* pp. 253–81.

26. A.E. Buchanan, "Deriving Welfare Rights from Libertarian Rights," in *Income Support,* pp. 233–46.

27. Some Marxians simply define 'exploitation' (or at least 'exploitation of the worker by the capitalist') as "the expropriation of surplus value produced by the worker." "Surplus value" here is the amount of value produced by the worker over and above the amount of value which the capitalist pays him for the use of his labor power; according to Marx, this latter amount tends to be only enough to pay for subsistence of the worker and his family. Nozick (*Anarchy, State, and Utopia,* p. 253) raises two objections to this view of exploitation: (a) it rests upon the labor theory of value (according to which the value of all commodities depends upon the amount of "socially necessary labor-time" required to produce them) and that theory is incorrect; and (b) the mere fact that the worker does not get back the full amount of value he produces (or the equivalent say, in money, of the goods he produces) is no reason to say he is exploited, since the workers will not get back the full value of their product in any society in which there is investment or in which those able to work subsidize those who cannot. What Nozick fails to see is that some Marxian views of exploitation, including those examined later in this section, do *not* rest upon the labor theory of value and do *not* claim that exploitation exists wherever the worker does not get back the full value of what he produces. Further, Nozick is unaware of the fact that Marx himself repudiated this conception of exploitation because he recognized that investment and subsidization of those unable to work were necessary and desirable and that wherever they occur the workers will not get back the full value of their product. (See A. E. Buchanan, *Marx and Justice,* chap. 3).

Two more recent attempts to develop a formal Marxian theory of exploitation deserve mention here. One is offered by R. P. Wolff in "A Critique and Reinterpretation of Marx's Labor Theory of Value," pp. 89–120; and in Wolff, "Reply to Roemer," *Philosophy and Public Affairs* vol. 12, no. 1 (1982):85–88. The other is that of J. E. Roemer, "Property Relations vs. Surplus Value in Marxian Exploitation," pp. 281–313; and in Roemer, "R. P. Wolff's Reinterpretation of Marx's Labor Theory of Value: Comment," pp. 71–83. Both Wolff and Roemer concentrate on developing formal models to capture what they take to be the most important insights of Marx's charge that capitalism is exploitative. But neither attempts a sustained investigation of the question with which we are concerned: Granted a particular conception of exploitation, what is *morally wrong* about exploitation? Wolff seems to espouse the naive Marxian view which Nozick criticized when he says that the exploitation of the worker in capitalism consists in the fact that there is "extraction of surplus value from the workers." The novelty of Wolff's position lies, it appears, not in his definition of exploitation, but rather in his account of the *locus* of exploitation: it "takes place in the interaction between the spheres of production and circulation," rather than exclusively in production or exclusively in circulation, as some Marxians have held ("A Critique and Reinterpretation of Marx's Labor Theory of Value," p. 114). Wolff offers no moral theory of exploitation.

Roemer rejects any attempt to define Marxian exploitation as a maldistribution of products or of income. Exploitation, according to Roemer is a matter of the maldistribution of *property,* that is, alienable, income-generating assets. He contends that exploitation exists whenever there is some segment of the population, *A,* who "would be better off under a redistribution of assets in which everyone in the society were endowed with exactly the same amount of alienable assets, and if their complement in the society would be worse off (in terms of income) under this [re-] distribution." ("R. P. Wolff's Reinterpretation of Marx's Labor Theory of Value: Comment," p. 81). What is remarkable is that Roemer has simply stipulatively defined as exploitive any system in which property is not distributed strictly equally or in which, if property is distributed unequally, the worst off would be better off if property were redistributed in a more egalitarian fashion. In other words, Roemer simply asserts without argument that exploitation occurs in every society in which Rawls's Difference Principle, applied to property, is not satisfied. However, on p. 82 Roemer seems to offer an even more stringent definition of exploitation, namely, one which states that exploitation exists whenever there are *any inequalities* in the distribution of property (even those that work to the advantage of the worst off in the sense that they are better off under the inegalitarian system than under strict equality). "Hence, the recipe for ending Marxian exploitation . . . is to eliminate differential ownership . . . of the means of production!" Roemer does not provide a justification for either version of his definition of 'exploitation'. He does not explain what is morally wrong with inegalitarian distributions of property, nor does he explain why, even if such distributions are morally wrong, they are properly called exploitive. One clue to Roemer's implicit moral perspective is found in the following remark: "Thus certain inequalities may be to the benefit of the exploited, or the least well off. The Rawlsian theory views such inequalities as just. I think, however, *justice entails that incomes to individuals are deserved*" (italics added; "Property Relations vs. Surplus Value in Marxian Exploitation," pp. 309–10). This passage indicates that Roemer rejects the Difference Principle version of his property-relations definition of 'exploitation' and holds the stronger version according to which exploitation exists wherever strict equality in the distribution of property does not obtain. It also leaves him open to obvious objections: (1) he has failed to distinguish between desert and entitlement; (2) he has begged the central question of the theory of justice by assuming that justice requires strict equality; and (3) by claiming that justice requires strict equality even when inequality would benefit the worst off, Roemer has divorced justice from efficiency and from the rational self-interest of the worst off.

28.   Nozick, *Anarchy, State, and Utopia*, pp. 253–62.

29.   J. Feinberg, "Noncoercive Exploitation."

30.   G. A. Cohen argues that though individual proletarians (workers) in capitalism are not coerced to work or unfree not to work, they are *collectively unfree;* that is, "each is free only on condition that the others do not exercise their similarly conditional freedom." It is not at all clear, however, that the fact that a system produces "collective unfreedom" in Cohen's sense shows that the system should be condemned or even reformed. Cohen himself seems to realize this when he acknowledges that while some instances of "collective unfreedom" may be tolerable, "collective unfreedom" with respect to one's productive activities is not. This latter claim, however, is far from self-evident. In order to show that capitalism is gravely defective because it produces "collective unfreedom" with respect to the worker's productive activities, the Marxist must show the harmful consequences of this kind of unfreedom, since as Cohen admits, it is not the mere fact of unfreedom (in this peculiar sense) which makes the system unacceptable. My conclusion is that the price of Cohen's defense of the Marxist claim that the workers are unfree or coerced to work for the capitalist is that the charge that they are coerced or unfree becomes largely irrelevant to the question of whether capitalism ought to be abolished or not. See G.A. Cohen, "The Structure of Proletarian Unfreedom," pp. 3–33.

31.   K. Marx, *Capital*, vol. 1, p. 256, for example.

32.   For a critical survey of the literature that supports this interpretation of Marx, see Buchanan, *Marx and Justice*, chap. 4.

33.   I. M. Kirzner, *Competition and Entrepreneurship*, esp. chap. 1 and 2.

34.   D. Schweikart, *Capitalism or Worker Control?*, pp. 1–27.

35.   S. Arnold, "Capitalism and the Ethics of Contribution," forthcoming.

36.   For two influential discussions of Marx's theory of alienation, see S. Avineri, *The Social and Political Thought of Karl Marx*, pp. 65–123; and B. Ollman, *Alienation: Marx's Conception of Man in Capitalist Society*.

37.   In *Marx's Ethic of Freedom*, G. F. Brenkert provides an interpretation of Marx's view as a whole, including his theory of alienation, which emphasizes freedom.

38.   G. McCallum, "Negative and Positive Freedom," pp. 318–53. For a valuable overview of different conceptions of freedom, see Joel Feinberg, *Social Philosophy*, chap. 1.

39. For a fuller analysis of Marx's theory of alienation, see A. E. Buchanan, *Marx and Justice*, chap. 2.
40.   A. Smith, *Lectures on Justice, Police, Revenue, and Arms*, p. 258; cited in A. Smith, *The Wealth of Nations*, p. xxxiv.
41.   Hegel, *The Philosophy of Right*, ed. T. M. Knox (London, 1973), esp. pp. 105–122.
42.   D. Gauthier, "The Social Contract as Ideology," pp. 130–64.
43.   R. M. Titmuss, *The Gift Relationship: From Human Blood to Social Policy* (London, 1971).
44.   P. Singer, "Altruism and Commerce: A Defense of Titmuss Against Arrow," *Philosophy and Public Affairs*, vol. 2, no. 3 (1972): 312–19.
45.   R. B. McKenzie and G. Tullock, *The New World of Economics*, pp. 48–49.

Chapter 4

1.   O. Lange and F. M. Taylor, *On the Economics of Socialism*.
2.   For presentations of worker management market socialism models, see D. Schweikart, *Capitalism or Worker Control?* esp. pp. 48–171; B. Horvat, *The Political Economy of Socialism*, esp. pp. 235–62; and J. Vanek, *The General Theory of Labor-Managed Market Economies*, esp. pp. 1–16.
3.   The following statement by Schweikart is true only if "the socialist critique of capitalism" means "the *non*-Marxist socialist critique of capitalism": "It is these two institutions [private property and wage labor], *not* the market, that lie at the heart of the socialist critique of capitalism." See *Capitalism or Worker Control?* p. 43 (italics added).
4.   For an explanation and critique of Marx's assumptions about the noncompetitive, nonegoistic motivation of communist man, see A. E. Buchanan, *Marx and Justice*, esp. chaps. 5 and 6.
5.   In *The Constitution of Liberty*, F. A. Hayek provides a sustained critique of rationalism in political thought.
6.   L. Mises, "Economic Calculation in the Socialist Commonwealth," p. 130.
7.   V. Pareto, *Cours d'economie politique*, vol. II, pp. 364ff; E. Barone, "Il ministerio della produzione nello stats collettivista."
8.   Hayek, "The Present State of the Debate," in *Collectivist Economic Planning*, esp. pp. 208–10.
9.   Ibid., pp. 232–41.
10.   A recent supporter of Hayek who overlooks this reply is John Gray in "F. A. Hayek and the Rebirth of Classical Liberalism," pp. 32–33.
11.   Hayek, *Collectivist Economic Planning*, pp. 232–41.
12.   B. Ward, "The Firm in Illyria: Market Syndicalism," pp. 556–89.
13.   For a critique of Ward's claim that worker-managed market socialist firms will tend to underexpansion because they maximize net income per worker rather than net total income, see Vanek, *Labor-Managed Market Economies*, pp. 2–38.
14.   Schweikart, *Capitalism or Worker Control?* p. 52.
15.   For a clear and more detailed examination of efficiency arguments concerning both types of market socialism, as well as a perceptive survey of the literature on this topic, see D. D., Milenkovitch, "Is Market Socialism Efficient?" pp. 65–107.
16.   See, for example, Kai Nielsen's *Radical Egalitarianism* and R. G. Peffer's "Marx, Morality, and Metaethics" for attempts to develop a moral theory that could be used in support of market socialism, especially of the worker managment variety. Schweikart's book, *Capitalism or Worker Control?* does not purport to ground the worker management model in a systematically developed moral theory, but it begins the task.

Glossary

Aggregative Efficiency: A system is aggregatively efficient if and only if it utilizes all productive resources.

Assurance Problem: A barrier to successful collective action or to the production of a public good that arises when all or some individuals decide not to contribute to the good in question because they lack adequate assurance that enough others will contribute.

Cost: The value of the most preferred alternative not taken.

Distributive Pareto Optimality Principle: A distributional state, S^1, of a system, is distributively Pareto Optimal if and only if there is no feasible alternative distributional state, S^2, of that system in which at least one individual is better off than in S^1 and no one is worse off than in S^1.

Externality: A neighborhood or third-party effect of an exchange (see chapter 1).

Free-Rider Problem: A barrier to successful collective action or to the production of a public good that arises because all or some individuals attempt to take a free ride on the contribution of others. Noncontributors reason as follows: Either enough others will contribute to achieve the good or they will not, regardless of whether I contribute or not; but if the good is achieved, I will benefit from it even if I don't contribute. Consequently, since contributing is a cost, I should not contribute.

Interpersonal Utility Comparisons: Judgments that rank the well-being, or happiness, or satisfaction of one individual with the well-being, happiness, or satisfaction of others.

Intersystemic Efficiency Comparisons: Judgments that rank the efficiency of one socioeconomic system with the efficiency of another socioeconomic system (where "efficiency" is understood according to the Paretian Principles or according to the notion of productivity).

Libertarianism: A political morality or normative political philosophy according to which force can only be justifiably used (by individuals or the state) to prevent or redress violations of negative rights—rights against physical harm, theft, and fraud.

Marginal Cost: The additional cost of producing or consuming one more unit of a good or service.

Marginal Productivity: The additional amount of output that can be achieved by a unit increase of inputs.

Market Capitalism: (or Capitalism): A socioeconomic system in which all or most of the means of production are privately owned and in which the market, including a market for labor power, plays a major role in coordinating activity for production, allocation, and distribution.

Market Equilibrium: A state of a market in which the total quantity of goods supplied equals the total quantity of goods demanded.

Market Socialism: A socioeconomic system in which the market plays a major role in coordinating production, allocation, and distribution, and in which there is public ownership of all or most means of production.

Monopoly: A condition of a market wherein one buyer or seller can unilaterally influence prices.

Pareto Optimality Principle (most inclusive form): A state, S^1, of a system is Pareto Optimal if and only if there is no feasible alternative state of that system, S^2, such that at least one individual is better off in S^2 than in S^1 and no one is worse off in S^2 than in S^1.

Pareto Superiority Principle: A state, S^1, of a system is Pareto Superior to an alternative feasible state, S^2, of that system if and only if at least one individual in S^1 is better off than in S^2 and no one is worse off in S^1 than in S^2.

Planned (or Nonmarket) Socialism: A socioeconomic system with public ownership of all or most of the means of production and in which a central plan is used to coordinate production, allocation, and distribution, in the absence of a significant role for the market.

Productive Pareto Optimality: A state, S^1, of a system is Productive Pareto Optimal if and only if there is no alternative state of that system, S^2, that would produce more of at least one good than is produced in S^1 without producing less of any other good that is produced in S^1.

Productivity: The ratio of outputs to a given set of inputs.

Public Goods: Any desired state of affairs that satisfies these conditions: (i) efforts of all or some members of a group are required to achieve the good; (ii) each member of the group regards his contribution as involving a cost; (iii) if the good is achieved, it will be produced in such a way as to be available to all members of the group, including noncontributors (jointness of supply); and (iv) if the good is produced it will be impossible or unfeasible to exclude noncontributors from partaking of it. (If, in addition, one individual's consumption of the good does not decrease the amount of the good available to others at all, the good is a *pure* public good.)

Socialism: A socioeconomic system in which the means of production are entirely or for the most part publicly owned.

Transaction Costs: The costs of making exchanges, including the costs of formulating bargains and contracts, and the costs, in terms of delays and losses of opportunities for mutually advantageous exchanges, of strategic behavior (bluffing, holding out for higher or lower prices, threatening to break off negotiations, and so forth).

Utilitarianism: A purportedly comprehensive moral theory that defines the good as utility (happiness, satisfaction) and that defines the right as that which maximizes that good. *Act Utilitarianism* defines *rightness* in terms of acts: An act is right if and only if it is that action among those available to the agent that maximizes (or can reasonably be expected to maximize) overall utility. *Rule Utilitarianism* defines *rightness* in terms of rules: a rule is right if and only if it is a member of a set of rules which, if generally acted on, will maximize overall utility.

Bibliography

Alchian, A., and Allen, W. R. *Exchange and Production: Competition, Coordination, and Control.* 2d rev. ed. Belmont, Calif.: Wadsworth, 1977.

Arnold, S. "Capitalism and the Ethics of Control." *Canadian Journal of Philosophy,* forthcoming.

Arrow, K. J. *Social Choice and Individual Values.* New Haven: Yale University Press, 2d rev., 1970.

Arthur, J., and Shaw, W. H., eds. *Justice and Economic Distribution.* Englewood Cliffs, N.J.: Prentice-Hall, 1978.

Avineri, S. *The Social and Political Philosophy of Karl Marx.* Cambridge, Eng.: Cambridge University Press, 1968.

Barone, E. "Il ministerio della produzione nello stats colletivista," *Giornale degli Economisti,* 1908 [The Ministry of Production in the Collectivist State], in F. A. Hayek, *Collectivist Economic Planning.* New York: Kelly, 1967.

Barry, B. *The Liberal Theory of Justice.* Oxford: Oxford University Press, 1973.

Baumol, W. J. *Welfare Economics and the Theory of the State.* Cambridge, Mass.: Harvard University Press, 1952. Reprint. 1965.

Baumol, W. J., and Blinder, A. S. *Economics: Principles and Policies.* 2d rev. ed. New York: Harcourt, Brace, & Jovanovitch, 1982.

Becker, L. *Property Rights: Philosophical Foundations.* Boston: Routledge & Kegan Paul, 1977.

Bedau, H. *Justice and Equality.* Englewood Cliffs, N.J.: Prentice Hall, 1971.

Bergson, A. *Essays in Normative Economics.* Cambridge, Mass.: Harvard University Press, 1966.

Berlin, I. *Four Essays on Liberty.* Oxford: Oxford University Press, 1969.

Bettleheim, C. *Economic Calculation and Forms of Property.* New York: Monthly Review Press, 1975.

Blaug, M. *Economic Theory in Retrospect.* 3d. rev. Cambridge, Eng.: Cambridge University Press, 1978.

Blocker, H. G., and Smith, E., eds. *John Rawls' Theory of Social Justice.* Athens, Ohio: Ohio University Press, 1980.

Brandt, R. B., ed. *Social Justice.* Englewood Cliffs, N.J.: Prentice-Hall, 1962.

_____ . *A Theory of the Good and the Right.* Oxford: Oxford University Press, 1979.

Brenkert, G. F. *Marx's Ethic of Freedom.* London: Routledge & Kegan Paul, 1983.

Brock, D. W. "Recent Work in Utilitarianism." *American Philosophical Quarterly,* vol. 10, no. 4 (October 1973):245–49.

Brody, B. *Ethics and Its Applications.* New York: Harcourt, Brace, & Jovanovitch, 1983.

Browning, E. K., and Browning, J. M. *Microeconomic Theory and Applications.* Boston: Little & Co., 1983.

Buchanan, A. E. "The Fetishism of Democracy: A Reply to Professor Gould." *Journal of Philosophy*, vol. LXXVII, no. 11 (1980):729–31.

———. "Deriving Welfare Rights from Libertarian Rights." In *Income Support*, edited by P. G. Brown, C. Johnson, and P. Vernier. Totowa, N.J.: Rowman & Allenheld, 1981, pp. 233–46.

———. *Marx and Justice: The Radical Critique of Liberalism.* Totowa, N.J.: Rowman & Allenheld, 1982.

———. "Marx on Democracy and the Obsolescence of Rights." *South African Journal of Philosophy*, vol. 2, no. 3 (1983):130–35.

———. "The Right to a Decent Minimum of Health Care." *Philosophy and Public Affairs*, vol. 13, no. 1 (Winter 1984):55–78.

———. "What's So Special About Rights?" *The Journal of Social Philosophy and Policy*, vol. 2, no. 1 (1984):61–83.

Buchanan, J. M. *The Demand and Supply of Public Goods.* Chicago: University of Chicago Press, 1968.

———. *The Limits of Liberty: Between Anarchy and Leviathan.* Chicago: University of Chicago Press, 1974.

———. "Order Defined in the Process of Its Emergence." *Literature of Liberty*, vol. V, no. 4 (Winter 1982):5.

Buchanan, J. M., and Tullock, G. *The Calculus of Consent.* Ann Arbor: University of Michigan Press, 1962.

Coase, R. H. "The Problem of Social Cost." *The Journal of Law and Economics* 3 (October 1960):1–33.

Cohen, G. A. "Labor, Leisure, and a Distinctive Contradiction of Advanced Capitalism." In *Markets and Morals*, edited by G. Dworkin, G. Bermant, and P. G. Brown. Washington, D.C.: Hemisphere Publishing Co., 1977, pp. 107–36.

———. *Karl Marx's Theory of History: A Defense.* Oxford: Oxford University Press, 1978.

———. "Robert Nozick and Wilt Chamberlain: How Patterns Preserve Liberty." In *Justice and Economic Distribution*, edited by J. Arthur and W. H. Shaw. Englewood Cliffs, N.J.: Prentice-Hall, 1978, pp. 246–62.

———. "The Labor Theory of Value and the Concept of Exploitation." *Philosophy and Public Affairs*, vol. 8, no. 4 (1979):338–60.

———. "The Structure of Proletarian Unfreedom." *Philosophy and Public Affairs*, vol. 12, no. 1 (Winter 1983):3–33.

Cohen, M., Nagel, T., and Scanlon, T., eds. *Marx, History, and Justice.* Princeton, N.J.: Princeton University Press, 1980.

Coleman, J. L. "Efficiency, Exchange and Auction: Philosophic Aspects of the Economic Approach to Law," Special Issue, *California Law Review:* Jurisprudence and Social Policy Program, vol. 68, no. 2 (1980):221–49.

———. "Efficiency, Utility, and Wealth Maximization," Special Issue, *Hofstra Law Review:* Efficiency as a Legal Concern, vol. 8, no. 3 (1980):509–51.

———. "Economics and the Law: A Critical Review of the Foundations of the Economic Approach to Law." *Ethics* 94 (July 1984):645–79.

Comisso, E. T. *Worker's Control Under Plan and Market.* New Haven: Yale University Press, 1979.

Conn, D. "Toward a Theory of Optimal Economic Systems." *Journal of Comparative Economics* 1 (1977):325-50.

———. "The Evaluation of Centrally Planned Economic Systems: Methodological Precepts." In *Comparative Economic Systems: An Assessment of Knowledge, Theory and Method*, edited by A. Zimbalist. Boston: Academic Press, 1984, pp. 15–46.

Cowan, J. L. *The Concept of Pleasure.* London: Macmillan, 1968.

Dahl, R. A., and Linblom, C. E., *Politics, Economics, and Welfare.* Chicago: University of Chicago Press, 1953.

Daniels, N. "Equal Liberty and Unequal Worth of Liberty." In *Reading Rawls*, edited by N. Daniels. New York: Basic Books, n.d. pp. 253–81.

———. *Reading Rawls.* New York: Basic Books, n.d.

Demsetz, H. "Toward a Theory of Property Rights." *American Economic Review*, vol. 57 (May 1964):347–59.

Dobb, M. *Welfare Economics and the Economics of Socialism: Toward a Commonsense Critique.* Cambridge, Eng.: Cambridge University Press, 1969.

Dworkin, G., Bermant, G., and Brown, P.G., eds. *Markets and Morals.* Washington, D.C.: Hemisphere Publishing Co., 1977.

Feinberg, J. *Social Philosophy.* Englewood Cliffs, N.J.: Prentice-Hall, 1973.

———. "Justice and Personal Desert." In *Doing and Deserving*, edited by J. Feinberg. Princeton, N.J.: Princeton University Press, 1970, pp. 55–87.

———. "Noncoercive Exploitation." In *Paternalism*, edited by R. E. Sartorius. St. Paul, Minn.: University of Minnesota Press, 1983, pp. 201–35.

———. "The Moral and Legal Responsibility of the Bad Samaritan." *Criminal Justice Ethics: Proceedings of the Eleventh World Congress of Law and Social Philosophy*, forthcoming.

Feldman, A. *Welfare Economics and Social Choice Theory.* Dordrecht, Holland: Martinus Nijhoff, 1980.

Ferguson, C. E., and Gould, J. P. *Microeconomic Theory*, 4th ed. rev. Homewood, Ill.: Richard D. Irwin, Inc., 1975.

Frankena, W. K. *Ethics*, 2d ed. rev. Englewood Cliffs, N.J.: Prentice-Hall, 1973.

Friedman, D. "Health on the Market," unpublished.

Friedman, M. *Capitalism and Freedom.* Chicago: University of Chicago Press, 1962.

Gauthier, D. "The Social Contract as Ideology." *Philisophy and Public Affairs*, vol. 6, no. 2 (1978):130–64.

Gramsci, A. *Prison Notebooks: Selections.* Hoare, Q., and Smith, G., eds. New York: International Publishing Co., 1971.

Gray, J. "F. A. Hayek and the Rebirth of Classical Liberalism." *Literature of Liberty* (Winter 1982):19–66.

Gregory, P. R., and Stuart, R. C. *Comparative Economic Systems.* Boston: Houghton-Mifflin, 1980.

Hayek, F. A. *Individualism and the Economic Order.* Chicago: University of Chicago Press, 1948.

———. *The Constitution of Liberty.* Chicago: University of Chicago Press, 1960.

———. *Collectivist Economic Planning.* New York: Kelley, 1967.

Hobbes, T. *Leviathan*, Parts I and II. Indianapolis: Bobbs-Merrill, 1958.

Hofstadter, R. *Social Darwinism in American Thought, 1860–1915.* Philadelphia: Beacon Press, 1944.

Holmstrom, N. "Exploitation." *Canadian Journal of Philosophy*, vol. VII, no. 2 (1977): 353–69.

Horvat, B., Markovic, M., and Supek, R., eds. *Self-Governing Socialism*, 2 vols. White Plains, N.Y.: M. E. Sharpe, 1975.

Husami, Z. "Marx on Distributive Justice." *Philosophy and Public Affairs*, vol. 8, no. 1 (1978):27–64.

Kamenka, E. *The Ethical Foundations of Marxism.* Boston: Routledge & Kegan Paul, 1962.

Kirzner, I. M. *Competition and Entrepreneurship.* Chicago: University of Chicago Press, 1973.

Kuperberg, M., and Beitz, C., eds. *Law, Economics, and Philosophy: A Critical Introduction with Application to the Law of Torts.* Totowa, N.J.: Rowman & Allenheld, 1983.

Lange, O. *Political Economy*, 2 vols. Oxford: Oxford University Press, 1971.

Lange, O., and Taylor, F. M. *On the Economics of Socialism*, edited by B. E. Lippincott. New York: McGraw Hill, 1956.

Lerner, A. *The Economics of Control.* New York: Kelly, 1946.

Lipsey, R. G., and Steiner, P. O. *Economics.* New York: Harper & Row, 1966.

Locke, J. *Second Treatise of Civil Government*, edited by P. Laslett, 2d rev. ed. Indianapolis: Bobbs-Merrill, 1952.

MacPherson, C. B. *Democratic Theory: Essays in Retrieval.* London: Oxford University Press, 1973.

McCallum, G. "Negative and Positive Freedom." *Philosophical Review* LXXVI (1967):318–53.

McKenzie, R. B., and Tullock, G. *Modern Political Economy.* New York: McGraw-Hill, 1978.
_____ . *The New World of Economics.* Homewood, Ill.: Richard D. Irwin, Inc, 1978.
Marx, K. *Capital,* 3 vols. New York: International Publishers, 1956.
_____ . *A Contribution to the Critique of Political Economy.* N.Y.: International Publishers, 1970.
_____ . *Grundrisse.* N. Martin, transl. New York: Random House, 1974.
Marx, K., and Engels, F. *The German Ideology: Parts I and III* (1845–46). New York: International Publishers, 1947.
Mandeville, B. *Fable of the Bees: Or Private Vices, Public Benefits,* 2 vols. Oxford: 1924.
Milenkovitch, D. D. "Is Market Socialism Efficient?" In *Comparative Economic Systems: An Assessment of Knowledge, Theory, and Method,* edited by A. Zimbalist. Boston: 1984, pp. 65–107.
Milliband, R. *Marxism and Politics.* Oxford: Oxford University Press, 1977.
Mises, L. "Economic Calculation in the Socialist Commonwealth." In *Collectivist Economic Planning,* edited by F. A. Hayek. New York: Kelley, 1967, pp. 87–130.
Mueller, D. *Public Choice.* Cambridge, Eng.: Cambridge University Press, 1979.
Murphy, J. G., and Coleman, J. L. *The Philosophy of Law: An Introduction to Jurisprudence.* Totowa, N.J.: Rowman & Allenheld, 1984.
Nagel, T. "Libertarianism Without Foundations." *Yale Law Journal,* vol. 85 (1975).
Nelson, W. M. *On Justifying Democracy.* London: Routledge & Kegan Paul, 1980.
Nielsen, K. *Radical Egalitarianism.* Totowa, N.J.: Rowman & Allenheld, 1984.
Niskanen, W. *Bureaucracy and Representative Government.* Chicago: Aldine-Atherton, 1971.
_____ . "Bureaucrats and Politicians." *Journal of Law and Economics,* (December 1975):615–53.
North, D. C. *Growth and Welfare in the American Past: a New Economic History.* Englewood Cliffs, N.J.: Prentice-Hall, 1966.
North, D. C. and Thomas, R. P. *The Rise of the Western World: A New Economic History.* Cambridge, Eng.:Cambridge University Press, 1973.
Nozick, R. *Anarchy, State, and Utopia.* New York: Basic Books, 1974.
Okun, A. M. *Equality and Efficiency: The Big Trade-Off.* Washington, D.C.: Brookings Institution Press, 1975.
Ollman, B. *Alienation: Marx's Conception of Man in Capitalist Society.* Cambridge, Eng.: Cambridge University Press, 1971.
Olson, M. *The Logic of Collective Action.* Cambridge, Mass.: Harvard University Press, 1965.
Pareto, V. *Cours d'economie politique.* Lausanne: 1897.
Paul, J. ed. *Reading Nozick.* Totowa, N.J.: Rowman and Allenheld, 1978.
Peffer, R. G. "Marx, Morality, and Metaethics." Ph.D. dissertation, University of Arizona, 1984.
Perry, J., ed. *Personal Identity.* Berkeley: University of California Press, 1975.
Quinney, R. *Class, State, and Crime.* New York: Longman, 2d. rev., 1980.
Rawls, J. *A Theory of Justice.* Cambridge, Mass.: Harvard University Press, 1971.
Riker, W. H. and Ordeshood, P. C. *An Introduction to Positive Political Theory.* Englewood Cliffs, N.J.: Prentice-Hall, 1973.
Robbins, L. *An Essay on the Nature and Significance of Economic Science.* London: Darby Books, 1932.
Roemer, J. E. "Property Relations vs. Surplus Value in Marxian Exploitation." *Philosophy and Public Affairs,* vol. 11, no. 4 (1982):281–313.
_____ . "R. P. Wolff's Reinterpretation of Marx's Labor Theory of Value: Comments." *Philosophy and Public Affairs,* vol. 10, no. 1 (1982):71–83.
Rorty, A. O., ed. *The Identities of Persons.* Berkeley: University of California Press, 1976.
Rosseau, J. J. *A Discourse on the Origin of Inequality.* In *The First and Second Discourses,* edited by R. D. Masters. New York: St. Martin's Press, 1964.
Sartorius, R. E. *Individual Conduct and Social Norms.* Belmont, Calif.: Wadsworth, 1975.
Scanlon, T. M. "Nozick on Rights, Liberty, and Property." *Philosophy and Public Affairs,* vol. 6, no. 1 (Fall 1976).

Schweikart, D. *Capitalism or Worker Control?* New York: Praeger Press, 1980.

Schumpeter, J. A. *Capitalism, Socialism, and Democracy.* New York: Harper & Row, 1947.

Sen, A. K. *On Economic Inequality.* New York: Norton, 1973.

Sen, A. K., and Williams, B., eds. *Utilitarianism and Beyond.* Cambridge, Eng: Cambridge University Press, 1982.

Smith, A. *The Wealth of Nations,* edited by E. Cannan. New York: Pergamon, 1937.

———. *Lectures on Justice, Police, Revenue, and Arms,* ed. and Introduction and Notes by E. Cannan (1896), cited in A. Smith, *The Wealth of Nations,* edited by E. Cannan. New York: Pergamon, 1957.

Sterba, J. P. *Justice: Alternative Political Perspectives.* Belmont, Calif.: Wadsworth, 1980.

Stigler, G. J. "The Theory of Economic Regulation." *The Bell Journal of Economics and Management Science,* vol. 2 (1971).

Thurow, L. C. *Generating Inequality.* New York: Basic Books, 1975.

Tullock, G. *The Politics of Bureaucracy.* Washington, D.C.: Public Affairs Press, 1965.

Tullock, G., and McKenzie, R. B. *Modern Political Economy.* New York: McGraw Hill, 1978.

Vanek, J. *The General Theory of Labor-Managed Market Economics.* Ithaca, N.Y.: Cornell University Press, 1970.

Ward, B. "The Firm in Illyria: Market Syndicalism." *American Economic Review* 48 (September 1958):556–89.

———. *The Ideal Worlds of Economics.* New York: Random House, 1979.

Watson, D. S., and Getz, M. *Price Theory and Its Uses.* Boston: Houghton-Mifflin, 1981.

Wiles, P.J.D. *Economic Institutions Compared.* Oxford: Oxford University Press, 1977.

Wolff, R. P. "A Critique and Reinterpretation of Marx's Labor Theory of Value." *Philosophy and Public Affairs,* vol. 12, no. 1 (1982):85–88.

Wood, A. *Karl Marx.* London: Routledge & Kegan Paul, 1982.

Zajac, E. E. *Fairness or Efficiency: An Introduction to Public Utility Pricing.* Cambridge, Mass.: Ballinger Publishers, 1978.

Zimbalist, A., ed. *Comparative Economic Systems: An Assessment of Knowledge, Theory and Method.* Boston: Academic Press, 1984.

Index

market, 101; exploitation, 87–96; Lockean or libertarian, 53, 64–78; Marx and, 47–48; mutually advantageous arrangements, 47, 54, 62–64; nonmarket systems, 47–48; Paretian analysis, 4–13; Social Darwinist argument, 49–51; utilitarianism, 54–62

Motivation, 107–8; market socialism, 112–13

Mutually advantageous argument, 9, 47, 50–51, 62–64; moral arguments, 54

Nagel, Thomas, 66

Nonmarket social organizations, 29, 36, 48, 95, 125; interaction with market, 101–3

Nozick, Robert, 64–70

Parasitism and exploitation, 87, 90–93

Paretian concept of efficiency, 4–13, 125; equilibrium state, 85–86; intersystemic efficiency comparisons, 37–38, 41–43; Pareto Optimal, 4–13, 125; Pareto Superior, 3–14, 125; utilitarianism, 61

Pareto, Vilfredo, 4, 45, 110

Paternalism, 10–12

Perry, John, 40

Pleasure and satisfaction, 7–8

Pollution problems, 22–24

Power relations, 86

Preferences, satisfaction of, 9, 11, 26–31; Paretian analysis, 9–12, 42–43

Private property market system, 2–3, 80, 94–95, 104; alienation and, 99–101; exploitation, 93–95; Libertarian theories, 65–68; market socialism, 3, 115, 117; moral theories, 53, 65–78; unemployment and, 35–36; voluntary exchanges, 67–70. *See also* Capitalism

Productivity, 3, 6, 18, 27, 80–81, 125; incentives for, 86, 92–94; marginal, 125; Paretian analysis, 4–13, 125

Property: private (*see* Private property market system); rights, 2, 53, 86–87

Public goods problems, 53, 73–78, 126; assurance problem, 23; free-rider problem, 22–23; government intervention, 24–25; utilitarianism and, 55–56, 58

Public ownership, 108–9, 113, 115

Rationality, Paretian analysis, 12–13

Rawls, John, 62, 69

Resource allocation. *See* Allocation of resources

Rights, 3, 48; legal, 81–87; moral arguments, 48, 81–87

Risk-taking, 92–93

Rousseau, Jean-Jacques, 99

"Safety net," 59

Satisfaction and pleasure, 7–9

Savings and investments, 34–35

Say, J. B., 34

Schweikart, David, 116

Sexual behavior and market attitudes, 103

Singer, Peter, 102–3

Smith, Adam, 18, 36, 63, 80, 92, 100–103

Social Darwinists, 49–51

Social starting place, 69–70

Social systems, assessment of, 8–9, 117

Socialism, 63, 80, 87, 126; market (*see* Market socialism)

Soviet Union, 108–9; intersystemic efficiency comparisons, 26–37, 43, 45, 115; policy choices, 28–29. *See also* Market socialism

Specialization, 17

Taxes and taxation, 59, 67, 86

Taylor, Fred M., 104

Taylor-Lange model, 104–9; critique of, 110–13

Titmuss, Richard, 101–3

Totalitarianism, 48

Transaction costs, 14–15, 19, 126

Tullock, Gordon, 103

Unemployment, 5, 32–36; efficiency arguments, 5, 32–33; market socialism, 115–16

Utilitarianism, 8, 13, 54–62, 126; civil and political liberties, 48, 58, 62; criticisms, 61–62; externalities and, 55–56, 58; government intervention, 58–59; moral arguments, 54–62; mutual advantage arguments, 62–64; Paretian analysis, 61; production incentives, 58; welfare programs, 55

Utility, principle of, 9, 13, 62; interpersonal utility comparisons, 8–9; marginal, 56–58

Vaccination program, 22–23

Voluntary exchanges, 67–69, 88, 92–93

Votes and voting, 29–31; vote-bargaining, 31

Ward, Benjamin, 113–14

Wealth and income: distribution according to "desert," 51–53; redistribution, 66–67, 85–86; utilitarianism theory, 55–57

Welfare programs, 59, 66, 85–86; social Darwinist argument, 49–50

Well-being, 40–41; concept of, 11–12, 53; individual's preferences and, 26–31; preference-satisfaction ratios, 42–43

Women, exploitation of, 87

Worker control, 87–95, 100; market socialism, 104–9, 112–17

Yugoslav economy, 43, 104, 106, 116